Scholars Praise
The Books of Śrīla Prabhupāda

"I think the best feature of the Hare Kṛṣṇa movement is that it is providing scholars with excellent translations of the rarest books on *kṛṣṇa-bhakti.*"

Dr. Lawrence Shinn
Professor of Religion,
Oberlin College

"I have read Sri Bhaktivedanta Swami's books with great care, attention, and profound interest, and have found them to be of incalculable value to anyone who is curious about India's spiritual and cultural heritage. The author of these books displays on every page an astounding scholarship in the subjects treated, and also an understanding and ease of exposition of abstruse ideas, which are rarest gifts."

Dr. H. B. Kulkarni
Professor of English
and Philosophy,
Utah State University

"The publications of the Bhaktivedanta Book Trust are very valuable documents and will no doubt become classics for the English reader of Indian religious literature."

Dr. Jerry M. Chance
Chairman, Department of
Philosophy and Religion,
Florida A & M University

THE LAWS OF NATURE

BOOKS by
His Divine Grace A. C. Bhaktivedanta
Swami Prabhupāda

Bhagavad-gītā As It Is
Śrīmad-Bhāgavatam, Cantos 1–10 (12 volumes)
Śrī Caitanya-caritāmṛta (17 volumes)
Teachings of Lord Caitanya
The Nectar of Devotion
The Nectar of Instruction
Śrī Īśopaniṣad
Easy Journey to Other Planets
Kṛṣṇa, the Supreme Personality of Godhead (3 vols.)
Perfect Questions, Perfect Answers
The Path of Perfection
Teachings of Queen Kuntī
Kṛṣṇa, the Reservoir of Pleasure
The Science of Self-Realization
Dialectical Spiritualism
The Journey of Self-Discovery
A Second Chance
Conversations with Śrīla Prabhupāda (30 volumes)
Letters from Śrīla Prabhupāda (5 volumes)
Kṛṣṇa Consciousness: The Topmost Yoga System
Teachings of Lord Kapila, the Son of Devahūti
Search for Liberation
Life Comes from Life
The Perfection of Yoga
Transcendental Teachings of Prahlāda Mahārāja
Beyond Birth and Death
On the Way to Kṛṣṇa
Message of Godhead
The Laws of Nature: An Infallible Justice
Civilization and Transcendence
Vairāgya-vidyā
Rāja-vidyā: The King of Knowledge
Elevation to Kṛṣṇa Consciousness
Kṛṣṇa Consciousness: The Matchless Gift
Back to Godhead magazine (founder)
Geetār-gān (Bengali)
Bhakti-ratna-boli (Bengali)

A complete catalog is available upon request.

In North America:
The Bhaktivedanta Book Trust
3764 Watseka Avenue
Los Angeles, California 90034

In Europe:
The Bhaktivedanta Book Trust
P.O. Box 324, Borehamwood,
Herts. WD6 1NB, U.K.

In Australasia:
The Bhaktivedanta Book Trust
P.O. Box 262
Botany, N.S.W., Australia

THE LAWS OF NATURE

An Infallible Justice

His Divine Grace
A.C. Bhaktivedanta Swami Prabhupāda
Founder-*Ācārya* of the
International Society for Krishna Consciousness

THE BHAKTIVEDANTA BOOK TRUST
Los Angeles • London • Stockholm • Bombay • Sydney • Hong Kong

THE COVER: Whether rich or poor, exploiter or exploited, all are controlled by the laws of nature, which act infallibly to award us our just deserts. Behind these laws are the three material modes—goodness, passion, and ignorance—and above all stands Lord Kṛṣṇa, the supreme controller. Only He can cut the ropes of *karma* and release us from material bondage.

Readers interested in the subject matter of this book are invited by the International Society for Krishna Consciousness to correspond with its secretary at one of the following addresses:

International Society for Krishna Consciousness
3764 Watseka Avenue
Los Angeles, California 90034
U.S.A.

International Society for Krishna Consciousness
P.O. Box 324, Borehamwood
Herts. WD6 1NB
England
Telephone: 01-905 1244

International Society for Krishna Consciousness
P.O. Box 262
Botany
N.S.W. 2019
Australia

First printing, 1991: 140,000

Printed in the United States of America
The Bṛhat Mṛdaṅga Press

Color separations/prepress by
ProMedia Color Graphics
221 Pine St., Northampton, Mass. 01060

Library of Congress Cataloging-in-Publication Data

A.C. Bhaktivedanta Swami Prabhupāda, 1896–1977
The laws of nature : an infallible justice / A. C. Bhaktivedanta Swami Prabhupāda
p. cm.
Includes index.
ISBN 0-89213-272-8
1. Karma. 2. Reincarnation 3. Krishna (Hindu deity)
4. Upanishads. Īśopaniṣad—Criticism, interpretation, etc.
5. Puranas. Bhāgavatapurāṇa—Criticism, interpretation, etc.
I. Title.
BL2015.K3A22 1991
294.5'22—dc20 91—25869
CIP

CONTENTS

INTRODUCTION

Man prides himself on being a creature of reason, above the lowly beasts. Yet it seems that when he applies his reason to unlocking the secrets of nature for his benefit, he sinks deeper and deeper into a quagmire of intractable problems. The internal combustion engine gets us where we're going faster, but also results in choking air pollution, the greenhouse effect, and a dangerous dependence on oil. Harnessing the atom gives us cheap energy, but also leads to weapons of mass destruction, Chernobyl, and a rising tide of dangerous radioactive waste. Modern agribusiness produces a dizzying variety and abundance of food at the supermarket, but also results in the death of the family farm, the pollution of ground water, the loss of precious topsoil, and many other problems.

It's clear we're missing something in our attempts to harness the laws of nature for our own purposes. What is that "something"? We find out in the very first *mantra* of the *Īśopaniṣad,* the foremost of ancient India's books of wisdom known as the *Upaniṣads:* "Everything in this creation is owned and controlled by the Lord. One should therefore accept only those things necessary for himself, which are set aside as his quota, and one should not accept other things, knowing well to whom they belong."

In nature we see this principle at work. Nature's arrangement, set up by the Lord, maintains the birds and beasts: the elephant eats his fifty kilos per day, the ant his few grains. If man doesn't interfere, the natural balance sustains all creatures.

Any agriculturalist will tell you the earth can produce enough food to feed ten times the present human population. Yet political intrigues and wars, unfair distribution of land, the production of cash crops like tobacco, tea, and coffee instead of food, and erosion due to misuse ensure that millions go hungry, even in wealthy countries like the United States.

We must understand the laws of nature from the viewpoint of the Supreme Lord, who has created these laws. In His eyes all the earth's inhabitants—whether creatures of the land, water, or air—are His sons and daughters. Yet we, the human inhabitants, the "most advanced" of His creatures, treat these sons and daughters with great cruelty, from the practice of animal slaughter to destruction of the rain forests. Is it any wonder that we suffer an unending series of natural disasters, wars, epidemics, famines, and the like?

The source of our problem is the desire for sense gratification beyond the consideration of anyone else's rights. These rights are the rights of the child in relation to the father. Every child has the right to share the wealth of his father. So creating a brotherhood of all creatures on earth depends on understanding the universal fatherhood of God.

As we have seen, the Vedic literature declares that the Supreme Lord owns and controls the entire creation. Not a blade of grass moves without His sanction. He is the complete whole. Then what is our position? Just as a king is no king without subjects, God is no God without His servants. He is the supreme enjoyer, and we are meant to take part in His enjoyment through service to Him, not by trying to enjoy separately. He is omnipotent and thus completely independent. Our minute independence is a tiny reflection of His total independence. It is our misuse of that minute independence and our attempt to enjoy separate from Him that have resulted in our current predicament.

Why do we misuse our independence? Because we are ignorant of our real nature. The first lesson of the Vedic wisdom is that we are not bodies but rather spirit souls—minute particles of consciousness dwelling within the body and animating it. Just as a car is a machine that allows a driver to travel from point A to point B, the body is a machine that allows the spirit soul to act and to experience sensations and thoughts within the Lord's material nature. When we understand our true identity as spiritual beings, part and parcel of the Supreme Spirit, God, we understand that we are meant to serve Him just as the hand or foot serves the whole body.

Our problem, however, is that we forget our identity separate from the body and instead misidentify ourselves with it. If a person happens to be born in America he considers himself an American, if he is born in France he considers himself a Frenchman, and so on. We also identify ourselves according to our sex, race, creed, social status, etc. But all these qualities apply only to the body, not the soul. Therefore embracing them as our true identity causes us to forget the Lord and our relationship with Him, and to see ourselves as independent enjoyers of His material nature.

The Vedic literature explains that human activity, when devoid of service to the Lord, is governed by a subtle law known as the law of *karma.* This is the familiar law of action and reaction as it pertains to what we do in this world and the enjoyment or suffering we experience as a result. If I cause pain to another living being, then as surely as the wheel of life turns, I will be forced to suffer similar pain. And if I bring happiness to another, a like pleasure awaits me. At every second, with every breath, our activities in this material world cause enjoyment and suffering. To facilitate these endless actions and reactions, there has to be more than just one life. There has to be reincarnation.

Until recently the idea of reincarnation, while universally accepted in India and other Eastern countries, had found few adherents in the West. The Church banned the philosophy of reincarnation centuries ago. This is a long story dating as far back as the history of the early Christian Church between 300 A.D. and 600 A.D. Recounting this controversy is not within the scope of this book, but the denial of this important concept has left a void in the world view of the Western peoples.

However, in the last decade or so many thinkers in the West have begun to take the idea of reincarnation seriously. For example, Dr. Michael Sabom of Emory University Medical School has written a book entitled *Recollections of Death: A Medical Investigation* (1982), which details his studies confirming the out-of-body experiences reported by cardiac arrest patients. Sabom writes, "Could the mind which splits apart from the physical brain be, in essence, the soul, which continues to exist after the final bodily death, according to some religious doctrines?"

And Dr. Ian Stevenson, a psychiatrist at the University of Virginia, in his book *Twenty Cases Suggestive of Reincarnation* (1966), has documented and verified past-life memories in young children. Other studies using such methods as hypnotic regression indicate that the idea of reincarnation may soon gain acceptance among mainstream scientists in the West.

The Vedic literature makes reincarnation of the soul a central feature in its explanation of human destiny. And the logic is obvious when we consider a simple question like the following: Why is one child born to wealthy parents in the United States, while another is born to starving peasants in Ethiopia? Only the doctrine of *karma* and reincarnation—reward and punishment carried over many lifetimes—answers this question easily.

The Laws of Nature: An Infallible Justice has been compiled primarily from two sources. The first is a series of talks given on the *Śrī Īśopaniṣad* by His Divine Grace A. C. Bhaktivedanta Swami Prabhupāda (see "The Author," p. 84). Delivered in Los Angeles in the spring of 1970, these talks provide an illuminating account of how the universe really operates. The second source is Śrīla Prabhupāda's commentated translation of the *Śrīmad-Bhāgavatam.* From the Third Canto of this monumental work we here reproduce Chapter Thirty, titled "Description by Lord Kapila of Adverse Fruitive Activities." In this section we learn the fate of the sinful soul who transgresses the laws of God's nature and incurs punishment according to the law of *karma*.

In one of his *Īśopaniṣad* talks, Śrīla Prabhupāda says, "If you do good work, you will have so-called enjoyment in your next life—but you will remain bound up in the cycle of birth and death. And if you do bad work, then you will have to suffer the sinful reactions and also remain bound up in birth and death. But if you work for Kṛṣṇa, there are no such reactions, good or bad, and at the time of death you will return to Kṛṣṇa. This is the only way to break the bonds of *karma*."

And this is the only way for society as a whole to mitigate the sufferings mentioned earlier. While we are in this world there is no getting rid of suffering altogether, for, as the Vedic teachings recognize, this material world is by nature a place of suffering. Ultimately we are powerless in the midst of a vast array of natural forces. The hope, therefore, is to know and follow the will of the Supreme Lord, the master of nature. Only in this way can we transcend the laws of nature, end the cycle of reincarnation, and attain the perfection of life—love of God and a place in His kingdom.

CHAPTER 1

GOD AND THE LAW OF KARMA

Among the vast ancient Sanskrit writings known as the Vedas, the 108 Upaniṣads contain the philosophical essence. And among all the Upaniṣads, the Īśopaniṣad is considered the foremost. In the following essay, based on talks Śrīla Prabhupāda gave on the Īśopaniṣad in 1968, we learn the truth about the Supreme Lord, the laws governing His material and spiritual energies, and how to break free of the bondage of karma.

The *Īśopaniṣad* states that the Supreme Personality of Godhead is "perfect and complete." Part of the Lord's complete arrangement for this material world is his process of creation, maintenance, and destruction. Every living being in this material world has a fixed schedule of six changes: birth, growth, maintenance, the production of by-products, diminution, and destruction. This is the law of material nature. A flower is born as a bud. It grows, remains fresh for two or three days, produces a seed, gradually withers, and then is finished. You cannot stop this by your so-called material science. To try to do so is *avidyā,* ignorance.

Sometimes people foolishly think that by scientific

advancement man will become immortal. This is nonsense. You cannot stop the material laws. Therefore in the *Bhagavad-gītā* (7.14) Lord Kṛṣṇa says that the material energy is *duratyayā,* impossible to overcome by material means.

Material nature consists of three modes, or *guṇas: sattva-guṇa, rajo-guṇa,* and *tamo-guṇa,* or the modes of goodness, passion, and ignorance. Another meaning of *guṇa* is "rope." Rope is made by twisting fiber in a threefold process. First the fiber is twisted in three small strands, then three of them are twisted together, then again three of those are twisted together. In this way the rope becomes very strong. Similarly, the three modes of nature—goodness, passion, and ignorance—are mixed, after which they produce some by-product. Then they are mixed again, and then again. Thus they are "twisted together" innumerable times.

In this way the material energy binds you more and more. By your own efforts you cannot get out of this bondage, which is known as *pavarga. Pa-varga* is the fifth set of letters in the Sanskrit Devanāgarī alphabet. It contains the letters *pa, pha, ba, bha,* and *ma. Pa* stands for *pariśrama,* "hard labor." Every living entity in this world is struggling very hard to maintain himself and survive. This is called the hard struggle for existence. *Pha* stands for *phena,* "foam." When a horse works very hard, foam comes out of its mouth. Similarly, when we are tired from working very hard, our tongue may become dry and some foam forms in our mouth. Everyone is working very hard for sense gratification—so much so that foam is coming from their mouth. *Ba* represents *bandha,* "bondage." In spite of all our efforts, we remain bound up by the ropes of the material modes of nature. *Bha* stands for *bhaya,* "fear." In material life, one is always in a blazing fire of fear, since no one knows what will happen next. And *ma* represents *mṛtyu,* "death." All our hopes and plans for happiness and security in this world are ended by death.

So, Kṛṣṇa consciousness nullifies this *pavarga* process. In other words, by taking to Kṛṣṇa consciousness one attains *apavarga,* where there is no hard struggle for existence and no material bondage, fear, or death. *Pavarga* symptomizes this material world, but when you add the prefix *"a"* to *pavarga,* that means it is nullified. Our Kṛṣṇa consciousness movement is the path of *apavarga.*

Unfortunately, people do not know of these things, and therefore they are wasting their lives. This modern civilization is a soul-killing civilization; people are killing themselves because they do not know what real life is. They are simply living like animals. The animal does not know what life is, so he simply works under the laws of nature, undergoing gradual evolution. But when you get this human form of life, you have a responsibility to live in a different way. Here is a chance for you to become Kṛṣṇa conscious and solve all problems. But if you don't—if you continue to act like animals—you will again have to enter the cycle of birth and death and transmigrate through 8,400,000 species of life. It will take many, many millions of years to come back to the human form of life. For example, the sunshine you are seeing now you will not see again until after twenty-four hours. Everything in nature moves in a cycle. So if you lose this opportunity of elevating yourself, then again you must enter the cycle of transmigration. Nature's law is very strong. Therefore we are opening so many centers so that people may take advantage of this International Society for Krishna Consciousness and elevate themselves.

It is important to take to Kṛṣṇa consciousness immediately, because we do not know how much time is left before death. When your time in this body expires, no one can stop your death. The arrangement of material nature is so strong. You cannot say, "Let me remain." Actually, people sometimes request like that. When I was in Allahabad, an old friend who was very rich was dying. At that time he begged the doctor, "Can't you give me at least four more years to live? I have some plans which I could not finish." You see. This is foolishness. Everyone thinks, "Oh, I have to do this. I have to do that." No. Neither the doctors nor the scientists can check death: "Oh, no, sir. Not four years, not even four minutes. You have to go immediately." This is the law. So before that moment comes, one should be very careful to become realized in Kṛṣṇa consciousness. You should realize Kṛṣṇa consciousness very quickly. Before your next death comes, you must finish your business. That is intelligence. Otherwise you will suffer defeat.

The *Īśopaniṣad* states that whatever emanates from the complete whole—the Supreme Lord—is also complete in itself. Therefore if you want to take advantage of your life and become Kṛṣṇa conscious, there is complete facility. But you have to come to the point of taking up the practice. Kṛṣṇa consciousness is not theoretical; it is practical. All experiments have already been performed. So, as indicated in the *Īśopaniṣad,* there is a complete facility for the small complete units—ourselves—to realize the supreme complete, Kṛṣṇa. We are complete units, but we are small. For example, in a big machine there is a small screw, and the perfection of that small screw is to be fitted in its proper place. Then it has value. But if it becomes unscrewed from the machine and falls down on the floor, it has no value. Similarly, we are perfect as long as we are attached to Kṛṣṇa; otherwise we are useless.

To realize the complete means to realize what our relationship with the complete is. And all forms of incompleteness are experienced only on account of incomplete knowledge of the complete. We are thinking, "I am equal to God. I am God." This is incomplete knowledge. But if you know, "I am part and parcel of God, and therefore I am equal to God in *quality,*" that is complete knowledge. The human form of life is a chance to revive the complete manifestation of the consciousness of the living being. You can revive this complete consciousness by the process of Kṛṣṇa consciousness. But if you don't take advantage of this complete facility, you are killing yourself, committing suicide. As it is said in the *Īśopaniṣad*, "The killer of the soul, whoever he may be, must enter into the planets known as the worlds of the faithless, full of darkness and ignorance." So don't be the killer of your soul. Utilize the complete facility of your human life to become Kṛṣṇa conscious. That is your only business.

BREAKING THE BONDS OF KARMA

In conditioned life we are committing sins at every step, even without knowing it. The reason we are sinning unknowingly is that we have been in ignorance from our very birth. This ignorance is prominent despite so many educational institutions. Why? Because despite so many big, big universities, none of them is teaching *ātma-tattva,* the science of the soul. Therefore people remain in ignorance, and they continue to sin and suffer the reactions. That is stated in the *Śrīmad-Bhāgavatam* (5.5.3): *parābhavas tāvad abodha-jāto yāvan na jijñāsata ātma-tattvam.* This foolishness will continue until one comes to the platform of understanding self-realization. Otherwise, all these universities and institutions for imparting knowledge are a continuation of that same ignorance and foolishness. Unless one comes to the point of asking "What am I? What is God? What is this world? What is my relationship with God and this world?" and finds proper answers, one continues to be foolish like an animal and is subjected to transmigration from one body to another in different species of life. This is the result of ignorance.

So, the modern civilization is very risky. One may feel comfortable as a successful businessman or politician, or one may think oneself comfortable because of being born in a rich nation like America, but these statuses of life are temporary. They will have to change, and we do not know what kind of miseries we will have to suffer in our next life because of our sinful activities. So if one does not begin cultivating transcendental knowledge, then one's life is very risky. Suppose a healthy man is living in a contaminated place. Is his life not at risk? He may become infected by disease at any moment. Therefore we should work to dissipate our ignorance through cultivation of transcendental knowledge.

A good example of how we commit sins unknowingly is cooking. In the *Bhagavad-gītā* (3.13) Kṛṣṇa says that His devotees are freed from sin because they eat only the remnants of food that has been offered to Him. But, He says, those who cook for themselves eat only sin. The difference between cooking here in this temple and cooking in some ordinary house is that our cooking and eating are relieving us from sin, while the cooking and eating of a nondevotee are simply entangling him more and more in sin. The cooking appears to be the same, but this cooking and that cooking are different. Here there is no sin because the food is being cooked for Kṛṣṇa.

Anything you do outside the field of Kṛṣṇa conscious activities entangles you in the modes of nature. Generally, you are being implicated in sinful activities. Those who are a little more cautious avoid sinful activities and perform pious activities. But one who performs pious activities is also entangled. If a man is pious, he may take birth in a family that is very rich or aristocratic, or he may be very beautiful or get the opportunity to become very learned. These are the results of pious activities. But whether you are pious or impious, you have to enter into the womb of some mother. And that tribulation is very severe. That we have forgotten. Whether you take birth in a very rich and aristocratic family or from an animal womb, the pangs of birth, old age, disease, and death continue.

The Kṛṣṇa consciousness movement is meant to give you an opportunity to solve these four problems—birth, old age, disease, and death. But if you continue to act sinfully and eat sinfully, then these miseries will continue. Otherwise, you can nullify your sinful reactions by surrendering to Kṛṣṇa, as He states in the *Bhagavad-gītā* (18.66): "Just give up all your so-called religious practices and surrender unto Me. I shall protect you from all your sinful reactions." Part of surrendering to Kṛṣṇa is being careful not to eat anything that has not been offered to Him. That should be our determination. Even if we have committed some sin, by eating *prasādam,* food offered to Kṛṣṇa, we will counteract it. If we surrender to Kṛṣṇa in this way, He will protect us from sinful reactions. That is His promise.

And where does a surrendered devotee go at the time of death? Is he finished, as the voidists say? No. Kṛṣṇa says, *mām eti:* "He comes to Me." And what is the benefit of going there? *Mām upetya punar janma duḥkhālayam aśāśvatam nāpnuvanti:* "One who comes back to Me does not have to return to this miserable material world." That is the highest perfection.

The *Īśopaniṣad* states, "The killer of the soul, whoever he may be, must enter into the planets known as the worlds of the faithless, full of darkness and ignorance." Kṛṣṇa is a lion to the demons and a lamb to the devotees. The atheists say, "We have not seen Kṛṣṇa." Yes, you will see Kṛṣṇa—you will see Him as the lion of death when He ultimately comes to capture you: "Ow!" The atheist sees Kṛṣṇa as death. And the theist, or devotee, sees Kṛṣṇa as his lover, as gentle as a lamb.

Actually, everyone is engaged in Kṛṣṇa's service, either out of love or by force. One who is entangled in material life is engaged in Kṛṣṇa's service because he is forced to serve Kṛṣṇa's external, material energy. It is just like what we see with the citizens of the state: whether one is a law-abiding citizen or a criminal, one is subservient to the state. The criminal may say he doesn't care for the state, but then the police will force him to accept the authority of the state by putting him in prison.

Therefore, whether one accepts or rejects Caitanya Mahāprabhu's philosophy that every living entity is eternally the servant of Kṛṣṇa, one remains His servant. The only difference is that the atheist is being forced to accept Kṛṣṇa as his master, and the devotee is voluntarily offering Him service. This Kṛṣṇa consciousness movement is teaching people that they are eternal servants of God and should voluntarily offer Him service: "Don't falsely claim that you are God. Oh, you don't care for God? You have to care." The great demon Hiraṇyakaśipu also didn't care for God, and so God came and killed him. God is seen by the atheist as death, but by the theist as a lover. That is the difference.

If you are a devotee and understand this philosophy of spiritual life, you can live for a moment or you can live for a hundred years—it doesn't matter. Otherwise, what is the use of living? Some trees live for five hundred or five thousand years, but what is the use of such a life, devoid of higher consciousness?

If you know that you are Kṛṣṇa's servant and that everything belongs to Kṛṣṇa, you can live for hundreds of years doing your duties and there will be no karmic reaction. This is confirmed in the *Bhagavad-gītā* (3.9): *yajñārthāt karmano 'nyatrā loko 'yaṁ karma-bandhanaḥ.* "Except work for Kṛṣṇa, any work, whether good or bad, will bind you to this material world." If you do good work, you will have so-called enjoyment in your next life—but you will still remain bound up in the cycle of birth and death. And if you do bad work, then you will have to suffer the sinful reactions and also remain bound up in birth and death. But if you work for Kṛṣṇa, there are no such reactions, good or bad, and at the time of death you will return to Kṛṣṇa. This is the only way to break the bonds of *karma.*

KṚṢṆA, THE CONTROLLER AND OWNER OF ALL

In the *Īśopaniṣad,* the word *īśa* is used to describe the Supreme Personality of Godhead. *Īśa* means "controller." Do you think you are controlled or not? Is there any person anywhere within this universe who is not controlled? Can anyone say, "I am not controlled"? Nobody can say that. So if you are controlled, then why do you declare, "I am not controlled, I am independent, I am God"? Why this nonsense? Māyāvādī impersonalists claim, "I am God, you are God, everyone is God." But if they are controlled, how can they be God? Does this make any sense? God is never controlled; He is the supreme controller. So if somebody is controlled, immediately we should know that he is not God.

Of course, some rascals claim that they are not controlled. I know one such rascal who has a society and is preaching, "I am God." But one day I saw him with a toothache; he was moaning, "Ohhh!" So I asked him, "You claim that you are God, the supreme controller, but now you are under the control of a toothache. What kind of God are you?" So if you see someone who claims that he is God or that everyone is God, you should immediately know such a person is a number-one rascal.

Now, this is not to say that the living entities are not controllers to some extent. In the *Bhagavad-gītā* Lord Kṛṣṇa says that the living entities are His superior energy. Why are the living entities superior energy? Because they are conscious, whereas the material energy is not. Therefore the living entities can control the material energy to some extent. For example, all the paraphernalia in this temple has been made from matter: earth, water, fire, and air. But it was a living entity who molded the material energy into this paraphernalia for the purpose of worshiping Kṛṣṇa. Another example: before people came from Europe, this land of America was mostly vacant. The people who lived here before that did not fully exploit it. But the Europeans came and developed it into a country with great industries and roads.

So the superior energy, the living entities, can have some control over the material energy. That Kṛṣṇa explains in the *Bhagavad-gītā* (7.5): *yayedaṁ dhāryate jagat.* The importance of this material world is due to the living entities. A big city like Los Angeles, New York, or London is valuable as long as the living entities are there. Similarly, the body is valuable as long as the living entity—the soul—is there. Therefore the soul is superior to matter. But that superiority is being misused to exploit matter for sense gratification. That is conditioned life. We have forgotten that, although we are superior to matter, we are still subordinate to God.

The people of the modern civilization do not care for God because they are intoxicated with their superiority over matter. They are simply trying to exploit matter in different ways. But they are forgetting that all people—American, Russian, Chinese, Indian—are subordinate to God. They have forgotten Kṛṣṇa and want to enjoy this material world. That is their disease.

So, the duty of the devotee of the Lord is to invoke the people's Kṛṣṇa consciousness. The devotee explains to them: "You are superior to matter, but you are subordinate to Kṛṣṇa. Therefore you should not try to enjoy matter but rather use it for His enjoyment." For example, we have decorated this temple not for our sense gratification but for Kṛṣṇa's pleasure. What is the difference between us and ordinary people? They are decorating their apartment very nicely, and we are decorating our place very nicely—but the purpose is different. We are doing it for Kṛṣṇa, and they are doing it for themselves. Whether you decorate your personal apartment or Kṛṣṇa's temple, your superiority over matter remains, since you are utilizing matter for your purposes. But when you apply your intelligence toward utilizing matter for Kṛṣṇa's pleasure, your life is successful, whereas when you apply the same intelligence for your sense gratification, you become entangled in material nature and feel anxiety. Then you have to change bodies, one after another.

Kṛṣṇa is the supreme controller of both the inferior energy, matter, and the superior energy, the *jīvātmā*—ourselves. We are Kṛṣṇa's superior energy because we can control the material world, but that control is also conditional. We have only limited control over this material world. But Kṛṣṇa has control over us; therefore, whatever control we have, He has sanctioned. For example, a human being has manufactured this nice microphone using his intelligence. That means he has been able to control matter to a certain degree to fulfill his desires. But where has his intelligence come from? Kṛṣṇa has given man his superior intelligence. In the *Bhagavad-gītā* (15.15) Kṛṣṇa says, *sarvasya cāhaṁ hṛdi sanniviṣṭo mattaḥ smṛtir jñānam apohanaṁ ca:* "I am seated in everyone's heart, and from Me come remembrance, knowledge, and forgetfulness." Therefore the supreme controller is giving intelligence to the superior energy in the human form of body: "Do this. Now do that . . ." This direction is not whimsical. The person wanted to do something in his past life, but in his present life he forgets, and so Kṛṣṇa reminds him: "You wanted to do this. Here is an opportunity." So although you have superior intelligence, that is also controlled by Kṛṣṇa. If Kṛṣṇa gives you the intelligence, you can manufacture this nice microphone. Otherwise, you cannot. Therefore in every sphere of life we are controlled by Kṛṣṇa.

We can also see Kṛṣṇa's control on the universal level. For example, there are so many huge planets; this earth planet is only a small one. Still, on this planet there are big oceans like the Atlantic and Pacific, as well as big mountains and skyscraper buildings. Yet despite all this load, the earth is floating in the air just like a swab of cotton. Who is floating it? Can you float even a grain of sand in the air? You may talk about the law of gravity and so many other things, but you cannot control it. Your airplane is flying in the air, but as soon as the petrol is finished, it will immediately fall. So if it takes so many scientists to build an airplane that can float only temporarily in the air, is it possible that this huge earth is floating of its own accord? No. Lord Kṛṣṇa declares in the *Bhagavad-gītā* (15.13), "I enter into the material planets and keep them aloft." Just as to keep an airplane aloft a pilot has to enter it, so to keep this earth aloft Kṛṣṇa has entered it. This is the simple truth.

We have to take knowledge from Kṛṣṇa. We shouldn't accept any process of gaining knowledge except hearing from Kṛṣṇa or His representative. Then we will have first-class knowledge. If you find an authority who is representing Kṛṣṇa and who can speak on the subject matter, and if you accept the knowledge he gives, then your knowledge is perfect. Of all the processes for receiving knowledge, the least reliable is direct sense perception. Suppose someone asks, "Can you show me God?" That means he wants to experience everything directly. But this is a second-class process for gaining knowledge, because our senses are imperfect and we are prone to make mistakes. Suppose you need some gold but you don't know where to purchase it. So you go to a proprietor of a hardware store and ask, "Do you have any gold in stock?" He will immediately understand that you are a first-class fool because you have come to purchase gold in a hardware store. Therefore he will try to cheat you. He will give you a piece of iron and say, "Here is gold." Then what will you say? Will you accept that iron as gold? Because you do not know what gold is and have gone to a hardware store to purchase it, you will get a piece of iron and be cheated. Similarly, rascals who demand that they be shown God do not know what God is, and therefore they are being cheated by so many bogus spiritual leaders who claim that *they* are God. That is happening.

If you want to purchase gold, you must have at least some preliminary knowledge of what gold is. Similarly, if you want to see God, the first requirement is that you must know some of the basic characteristics of God. Otherwise, if you go to some rascal and he claims to be God and you accept him as God, you will be cheated.

Another question we should ask when someone says "I want to see God" is, "What qualification do you have to see God?" God is not so cheap that He can be seen by anybody and everybody. No, the Kṛṣṇa consciousness movement does not present any nonsense or cheap thing. If you want to see God face to face, then you must follow the rules and regulations. You must chant Hare Kṛṣṇa and purify yourself. Then gradually the time will come when you are purified and you will see God.

Still, even though in your present contaminated condition you are not qualified to see God, He is so kind that He allows you to see Him in His Deity form in the temple. In that form He agrees to be seen by everyone, whether or not one knows He is God. The Deity is not an idol; it is not imagination. The knowledge of how to construct the Deity and install Him on the altar is received from the scripture and the superior *ācāryas,* or spiritual masters. Therefore the authorized Deity in the temple is Kṛṣṇa Himself and can fully reciprocate your love and service.

With your present blunt material senses, however, you cannot immediately perceive God's spiritual form, name, qualities, pastimes, and paraphernalia. And because people in the present civilization have no power to understand God, nor are they guided by some person who can help them understand God, they have become godless. But if you read Vedic scriptures like the *Īśopaniṣad* and *Bhagavad-gītā* under superior guidance and follow the rules and regulations, eventually God will be revealed to you. You cannot see God or understand God by your own endeavor. You have to surrender to the process by which God can be known. Then He will reveal Himself. He is the supreme controller; you are being controlled. So how can you control God? "O God, come here. I want to see You." God is not so cheap that by your order He will come and be seen by you. No, that is not possible. You must always remember, "God is the supreme controller and I am controlled. So if I can please God by my service, then He will reveal Himself to me." That is the process of knowing God.

Ultimately, this process leads to love of God. That is real religion. It doesn't matter whether you follow the Hindu, Muslim, or Christian religion: if you are developing love of God, then you are perfect in your religion. And what kind of love should we develop for God? It must be without any selfish motivation— "O Lord, I love you because You supply me so many nice things. You are my order supplier." No, we should not have this sort of love for God. It should not depend on any exchange.

Lord Caitanya Mahāprabhu taught, "O Lord! Whether You trample me under Your feet or embrace me or leave me brokenhearted by not being present before me, that does not matter. You are completely free to do anything, for You are my worshipable Lord unconditionally." That is love. We should think, "God may do whatever He likes, yet I will still love Him. I don't want anything in exchange." That is the sort of love Kṛṣṇa wants. That is why He is so fond of the *gopīs*. In the *gopīs'* love there is no question of business exchanges—"Give me this, then I will love You." Their love was pure, unalloyed, without any impediment. If you try to love God in this way, nothing in the whole world can check you. You only have to develop your eagerness—"Kṛṣṇa! I want You." That's all. Then there is no question of being stopped. In any condition your love will increase. If you attain that state, you will feel fully satisfied. It is not that God wants you to love Him for His benefit. It is for your benefit. If you do otherwise, you will never be happy.

GOD AND HIS ENERGIES

The *Īśopaniṣad* explains that whatever we see, whether animate or inanimate, is controlled by the

Supreme Lord. Lord Kṛṣṇa says the same thing in the *Bhagavad-gītā* (9.10)—that His energies are managing everything. And the *Viṣṇu Purāṇa* confirms, *eka-deśa-sthitasyāgner jyotsnā vistārinī yathā:* "As heat and light are distributed all around by a fire situated in one place, so the whole creation is a manifestation of energies expanded from the Supreme Lord." For example, the sun is in one place, but it is distributing its heat and light all over the universe. Similarly, the Supreme Lord is distributing His material and spiritual energies all over the creation.

The spiritual energy is present in this temporary material world, but it is covered by the material energy. For example, the sun is always shining in the sky—no one can stop the sun from shining—but it is sometimes covered by a cloud. When this happens, the sunshine on the ground is dim. The more the sun is covered, the dimmer the sunlight. But this covering of the sun is partial. All the sunshine cannot be covered; that is not possible. An insignificant portion of the sunshine may be covered by a cloud. Similarly, this material world is an insignificant portion of the spiritual world that is covered by the material energy.

And what is the material energy? The material energy is just another form of the spiritual energy. It manifests when there is an absence of spiritual activity. Again the analogy of the sun and the cloud: What is a cloud? It is an effect of the sunshine. The sunshine evaporates water from the sea, and a cloud is formed. So the sun is the cause of the cloud. Similarly, the Supreme Lord is the cause of this material energy, which covers our vision of Him.

In this way, two energies are working in this material world: the spiritual energy and the material energy. The material energy consists of eight material elements: earth, water, fire, air, ether, mind, intelligence, and false ego. These are arranged from the grosser to the finer. Water is finer than earth, fire is finer than water, etc.

So, the finer the element, the more powerful it is. For example, at the speed of the mind you can go many thousands of miles within a second. But even more powerful than the mind is the intelligence, and even more powerful than the intelligence is spiritual energy. What is spiritual energy? That is stated by Kṛṣṇa in the *Bhagavad-gītā* (7.5): *apareyam itas tv anyāṁ prakṛtiṁ viddhi me parām jīva-bhūtām.* "Beyond My inferior, material energy is another energy, which is spiritual. It comprises the living entities."

We living entities are also energy, but superior energy. How are we superior? Because we can control the inferior energy, matter. Matter has no power to act on its own. The big airplane can fly so nicely in the sky, but unless the spiritual energy—the pilot—is there, it is useless. The jet plane will sit in the airport for thousands of years; it will not fly unless the small particle of spiritual energy, the pilot, comes and touches it. So what is the difficulty in understanding God? If there are so many huge machines that cannot move without the touch of the spiritual energy, a living being, then how can you argue that this whole material energy works automatically, without any control? Who would put forward such a foolish argument? Therefore, those who cannot understand how this material energy is being controlled by the Supreme Lord are less intelligent. The godless men who believe that this material energy is working automatically are fools.

The statement of the *Īśopaniṣad* is that "Everything animate or inanimate is controlled and owned by the Supreme Personality of Godhead." Because He is the supreme controller, He is also the supreme proprietor. In our practical experience we see that the man who controls a business establishment is the proprietor. Similarly, since God is the controller of this material world, He is also its proprietor. This means that as far as possible we should engage everything in the Lord's service.

Then what about our own needs? That is explained in the *Īśopaniṣad:* "One should accept only those things necessary for himself, which are set aside as his quota, and one should not accept other things, knowing well to whom they belong." Kṛṣṇa consciousness means to understand things as they are. So if we simply understand these principles, we will be well situated in Kṛṣṇa consciousness.

THE POSITION OF KṚṢṆA

The *Īśopaniṣad* states, "Although fixed in His abode, the Personality of Godhead is swifter than the mind and can overcome all others running. The powerful demigods cannot approach Him. Although in one place, He controls those who supply the air and rain. He surpasses all in excellence." The *Brahma-saṁhitā* says something similar: *goloka eva nivasaty akhilātma-bhūtaḥ.* Although

Kṛṣṇa is always in Goloka Vṛndāvana, He is simultaneously in the hearts of all living beings.

Kṛṣṇa has no duties to perform in Goloka. He is simply enjoying in the company of His associates—the *gopīs*, the cowherd boys, His mother and father, His cows and calves, etc. He is completely free. And His associates are even freer than He is, because when they seem to be in danger, Kṛṣṇa feels some anxiety about how to save them. But His associates feel no anxiety. They simply think, "Oh, Kṛṣṇa is here. He will protect us." When Kṛṣṇa enacted His pastimes five thousand years ago in Vṛndāvana, India, He would go every day with His cowherd boyfriends and their calves and cows to play in the forest on the bank of the Yamunā River. And often Kaṁsa would send some demon to try to kill Kṛṣṇa and His friends. Yet the cowherd boys would continue enjoying their pastimes without anxiety because they were so confident of Kṛṣṇa's protection. That is spiritual life, which begins with surrendering to Kṛṣṇa.

Surrendering to Kṛṣṇa means having the strong faith that Kṛṣṇa will save us in any dangerous condition. The first step in surrendering is that we should accept whatever is favorable for devotional service. Then we should reject anything that is unfavorable for devotional service. The next stage is the confidence that in any situation Kṛṣṇa will protect us and maintain us. Actually, He is already giving protection and maintenance to everyone. That is a fact. But in *māyā* (illusion) we think that we are protecting ourselves, or that we are feeding ourselves.

For the devotees, Kṛṣṇa personally takes charge of their protection and maintenance. And for the ordinary living entities, Māyā-devī—Kṛṣṇa's external energy—takes charge. Māyā-devī is Kṛṣṇa's agent for punishing the conditioned souls. The situation is like what we see in the state: good citizens are taken care of by the government directly, while criminals are taken care of by the government through the prison department. In the prison house the government takes care that the prisoners get sufficient food, and that they get hospital treatment if they become diseased. The government cares for them—but under punishment.

Similarly, in this material world Kṛṣṇa has certainly arranged for our care, but also for our punishment. If you commit this sin, then slap. If you commit that sin, then kick. This is going on under the heading of the threefold miseries—those caused by our own body and mind, those caused by other living entities, and those caused by natural calamities under the supervision of the demigods. Unfortunately, instead of understanding that we are being punished for sinful activities, under the spell of *māyā* we are thinking that this kicking, slapping, and thrashing are accidental. This is illusion.

As soon as you take up Kṛṣṇa consciousness, Kṛṣṇa begins personally taking care of you. As He promises in the *Bhagavad-gītā* (18.66), "I will take care of you. I will save you from all sinful reactions. Do not worry." Because we have had so many lives in this material world, we are suffering under heaps of sinful reactions. But as soon as you surrender to Kṛṣṇa, He immediately takes care of you and nullifies all your sinful reactions. Kṛṣṇa says, "Don't hesitate." Don't think, "Oh, I have committed so many sins. How can Kṛṣṇa save me?" No. Kṛṣṇa is all-powerful. He can save you. Your duty is to surrender to Him and without any reservation dedicate your life to His service. Then Kṛṣṇa will save you without a doubt.

KṚṢṆA: A SEEMING PARADOX

The *Īśopaniṣad* states, "The Supreme Lord walks and does not walk. He is far away, but He is very near as well. He is within everything, and yet He is outside of everything." How can Kṛṣṇa walk and also not walk? As a crude example, consider how the sun at noontime shines on your head. Now, if you begin walking, you will see that the sun is accompanying you. About forty years ago, when I was a householder, I was once walking with my second son in the evening. He was four years old. All of a sudden he said, "O father, why is the moon following us?" You see? The moon and the sun are fixed in the sky, yet they seem to be moving with us. Similarly, if you are going on an airplane or a train, you will see that the moon or the sun is going with you. So if this is possible for the sun and the moon, why can't Kṛṣṇa also walk with you? "Although He is situated far away, He is very near as well." In other words, although Kṛṣṇa is in Goloka Vṛndāvana enjoying pastimes with His associates, He is simultaneously everywhere in this material world. In this way the Supreme Lord "walks and does not walk."

If Kṛṣṇa were not present here as well as in Goloka,

how could He accept the food the devotees offer Him? Don't think that Kṛṣṇa does not accept the devotees' offerings. He can stretch His hand immediately if one offers Him something with devotion. In the *Bhagavad-gītā* (9.26) Kṛṣṇa says, *tad ahaṁ bhakty-upahṛtam aśnāmi:* "Whenever someone offers Me something with faith and love, I accept it." People may ask, "Oh, Kṛṣṇa is far away in Goloka Vṛndāvana. How can He eat your offering?" Yes, He accepts it. Yes, He eats it—provided it is offered with love.

So, Kṛṣṇa is present everywhere, and He can manifest Himself anywhere immediately, but you must have the qualification to call Him. If you are actually a devotee, Kṛṣṇa will immediately come to protect you. The demon Hiraṇyakaśipu challenged his son, the devotee Prahlāda: "Where is your God? You say He is everywhere. Then is He in this column of my palace? You think your God is there? All right. Then I will kill Him." Hiraṇyakaśipu immediately broke the column. Then Kṛṣṇa came out of the column in His form as Nṛsiṁhadeva—half man and half lion—and killed the demon. That is Kṛṣṇa.

So Kṛṣṇa can manifest Himself anywhere because He is present everywhere. That is explained in the *Īśopaniṣad: tad antarasya sarvasya tad u sarvasyāsya bāhyataḥ*. "The Supreme Lord is within everything, and yet He is outside of everything as well." This Vedic *mantra* is proof that the Lord is everywhere. Whatever is said in the *Vedas* is a fact. Unless you accept the *Vedas* as axiomatic truth, you cannot make progress in Kṛṣṇa consciousness. In mathematics there are also many axiomatic truths—a point has no length or breadth, things equal to the same thing are equal to one another, etc. These are axiomatic truths, and we have to accept them if we want to learn mathematics. Similarly, the *Vedas* contain axiomatic truths, and we have to accept the *Vedas* as axiomatic if we want to make spiritual progress.

Sometimes the *Vedas* seem to contradict themselves, but still we have to accept all the Vedic injunctions. For example, according to Vedic injunction, if you touch the bone of an animal you immediately become impure and must take a bath. Now, a conchshell is the bone of an animal, but the conchshell is used in the Deity room, where everything must be spotlessly pure. You cannot argue, "Oh, you said that a bone is impure, and that as soon as you touch it you become impure. Still you are putting a conchshell in the Deity room?" No. There is no room for such an argument. You have to accept that while bones are impure, the conchshell is so pure that it can be used in the Deity room.

Similarly, you have to accept the spiritual master's order as axiomatic. There can be no argument. In this way you can make progress. You cannot argue about things that are inconceivable to you. You will only fail. You have to accept the Vedic injunctions and the orders of the spiritual master as axiomatic truth. This is not dogmatic, because our predecessor spiritual masters accepted this principle. If you argue with your spiritual master, you will never reach a conclusion. The argument will go on perpetually: you put some argument, I put some argument . . . That is not the process.

As the *Mahābhārata* says, *tarko 'pratiṣṭhaḥ śrutayo*

vibhinnā: Mere logic and argument can never come to a firm conclusion, and due to different countries and different circumstances, one scripture is different from another. Then *nāsāv ṛṣir yasya mataṁ na bhinnam:* As far as philosophical speculation is concerned, one philosopher puts forward some theory, then another philosopher puts forward another theory, and the theories always contradict each other. Unless you defeat another philosopher, you cannot be a famous philosopher. That is the way of philosophy. Then how can one learn the conclusive philosophical truth? That is stated: *dharmasya tattvaṁ nihitaṁ guhāyām.* The secret of the religious process is lying within the hearts of the self-realized souls. Then how do you realize it? *Mahājano yena gataḥ sa panthāḥ:* You have to follow in the footsteps of great spiritual personalities. Therefore we are trying to follow Lord Kṛṣṇa and Lord Caitanya. That is perfection. You have to accept the injunctions of the *Vedas,* and you have to follow the instructions of the bona fide spiritual master. Then success is sure.

THE LORD AND HIS ENERGY—ONE AND DIFFERENT

The *Īśopaniṣad* states, "One who always sees all living entities as spiritual sparks, in quality one with the Lord, becomes a true knower of things. What, then, can cause him illusion or anxiety?" This realization is Kṛṣṇa consciousness. There are different kinds of realization, but the devotee of Kṛṣṇa realizes the truth—that we are qualitatively one with the Lord but quantitatively different from Him. The impersonalists think that we are a hundred percent one with the Lord, or the Supreme Absolute Truth. But that is not a fact. If we were a hundred percent one with the Supreme Lord, then how have we come under the control of *māyā* (illusion)? The impersonalists cannot answer this question.

The real nature of our identity with the Supreme is described in the Vedic literature with the analogy of the sparks and the fire. The sparks of a fire have the same quality as the fire, yet they are different in quantity. But when the small spark leaves the fire and falls down in water, its fiery quality is lost. Similarly, when the infinitesimal soul leaves the association of the Lord and contacts the mode of ignorance, his spiritual quality becomes almost extinct. When a spark falls on the land instead of in the water, then the spark retains some heat. Similarly, when the living entity is in the quality of passion, there is some hope that he can revive his Kṛṣṇa consciousness. And if the spark drops onto dry grass, it can ignite another fire and regain all its fiery qualities. Similarly, a person who is in the mode of goodness can take full advantage of spiritual association and easily revive his Kṛṣṇa consciousness. Therefore one has to come to the platform of goodness in this material world.

Again, the analogy of the fire can help us understand the simultaneous oneness and difference of the Lord and His diverse energies. Fire has two main energies, heat and light. Wherever there is fire, there is heat and light. Now, the heat is not different from the fire, nor is the light—but still, heat and light are not fire. Similarly, the whole universe can be understood in this way. The universe is simply made up of Kṛṣṇa's energies, and therefore nothing is different from Kṛṣṇa. But still, Kṛṣṇa is separate from everything in the material universe.

So, whatever we see within the material or spiritual worlds is but an expansion of Kṛṣṇa's multifarious energies. This material world is an expansion of Kṛṣṇa's external energy (*bahiraṅgā śakti*), the spiritual world is an expansion of His internal energy (*antaraṅgā śakti*), and we living entities are an expansion of His marginal energy (*taṭasthā śakti*). We are *śakti,* energy. We are not the energetic.

The Māyāvādī philosophers say that because the energies are not outside of Brahman, the energetic, they are all identical with Brahman. This is monism. Our Vaiṣṇava philosophy is that the energy is simultaneously one with and different from the energetic. Again the analogy of the heat and fire: When you perceive heat, you understand that there is fire nearby. But this does not mean that because you feel some heat, you are *in* the fire. So the heat and the fire, the energy and the energetic, are one yet different.

So the Māyāvāda philosophy of oneness and our Vaiṣṇava philosophy of oneness are different. The Māyāvādīs say Brahman is real but that the energy emanating from Brahman is false. We say that because Brahman is real, His energy must also be real. That is the difference between Māyāvāda philosophy and Vaiṣṇava philosophy. One cannot claim that this material energy is false, although it is certainly temporary. Suppose we have some trouble. There are so many kinds of trouble pertaining to the body and mind and external affairs. That trouble comes and goes, but when we are undergoing it, it is certainly real. We feel the consequence. We cannot say it is false. The Māyāvādī philosophers say that it is false. But then why do they become so disturbed when they have some trouble? No, none of Kṛṣṇa's energies is false.

The *Īśopaniṣad* uses the word *vijānataḥ*—"one who knows"—to describe a person who understands the oneness and difference of the Lord and His energies. If one is not *vijānataḥ,* one will remain in illusion and suffer. But for one who knows, there is no illusion, no lamentation. When you are perfectly convinced that there is nothing except Kṛṣṇa and Kṛṣṇa's energies, then there is no illusion or lamentation for you. This is known as the *brahma-bhūta* stage, as explained in the *Bhagavad-gītā* (18.54): *brahma-bhūtaḥ prasannātmā na śocati na kāṅkṣati.* "One who is transcendentally situated in Brahman realization becomes fully joyful, and he never laments or desires to have anything."

For our sense gratification we are very eager to get things we do not have. That is hankering. And when we lose something, we lament. But if we know that Kṛṣṇa is the source and proprietor of the entire material energy, we understand that everything belongs to Him and that anything gained is given by Him for His service. Thus we do not hanker for the things of this world. Furthermore, if something is taken away by Kṛṣṇa, then what is the need for lamentation? We should think, "Kṛṣṇa wanted to take it away from me. Therefore, why should I lament? The Supreme Lord is the cause of all causes. He takes away, He also gives." When one is thus in full knowledge, there is no more lamentation and no more hankering. That is the spiritual platform. Then you can see everyone as a spiritual spark, as part and parcel of Kṛṣṇa, and as His eternal servant.

KṚṢṆA, THE SUPREME PURE

The *Īśopaniṣad* states that the Lord is "the greatest of all, unembodied, omniscient, beyond reproach, without veins, pure and uncontaminated." No sin can pollute Kṛṣṇa. Sometimes less intelligent persons criticize Kṛṣṇa: "Why did Kṛṣṇa engage in the *rāsa* dance, enjoying with other men's wives in the middle of the night?" Kṛṣṇa is God. He can do whatever He likes. Your laws cannot restrict Kṛṣṇa. For you there are so many restrictive laws, but for Kṛṣṇa there is no restrictive law. He can surpass all regulations.

Parīkṣit Mahārāja asked this same question of Śukadeva Gosvāmī: "Kṛṣṇa came to establish the principles of morality and religion. Then why did He enjoy the company of so many young girls who were the wives of others? This seems to be very sinful." Śukadeva Gosvāmī answered that Kṛṣṇa cannot be contaminated by sin; rather, whoever comes in contact with Kṛṣṇa, even with a contaminated mind, becomes purified. The sun is a good analogy: the sun cannot be contaminated; rather, if something contaminated is placed in the sunshine, it becomes purified. Similarly, you may approach Kṛṣṇa with any material desire and you will become purified. Of course, the *gopīs'* feelings toward Kṛṣṇa are not at all material. Still, as young girls they were captivated by His beauty. They approached Kṛṣṇa with the desire to have Him as their paramour. But actually, they became purified. Even demons can become purified by coming in contact with Kṛṣṇa.The demon Kaṁsa, for example, thought of Kṛṣṇa as his enemy. But he was also Kṛṣṇa conscious, always thinking, "Oh, how will I find Kṛṣṇa? I will kill Him." That was his demoniac mentality. But he also became purified. He got salvation.

The conclusion is that if we can somehow or other develop our Kṛṣṇa consciousness, we will immediately become purified of all sinful desires. Kṛṣṇa gives this chance to everyone.

BEYOND THE LIMITS OF THE BODY

When the *Īśopaniṣad* describes the Supreme Lord as "He who is the greatest of all, who is unembodied and omniscient," this shows the distinction between God and ourselves. We are embodied. Therefore my body is different from me. When I leave this body, it becomes dust. As the Bible says, "Dust thou art, and unto dust shalt thou return." But *I* am not dust; I am a spirit soul. Therefore *thou* means "the body."

Kṛṣṇa, however, is not embodied. This means there is no difference between His body and His soul. In other words, His body is pure spirit. Therefore He does not change His body. And because He does not change His body, He is omniscient—He remembers everything. Because we do change our material bodies, however, we forget what happened in our last birth. We have forgotten who we were, just as when we sleep we forget our body and our surroundings. The body becomes tired and rests; it becomes inactive. In contrast, in a dreamland I work, I go somewhere, I fly, I create another body, another environment. This we experience every night. It is not difficult to understand.

Similarly, in every life we create a different environment. In this life I may think I am an Indian. In my next life, however, I may not be an Indian—I may be an American. But even if I become an American, I may not be a man. I may be a cow or a bull. Then I would be sent to the slaughterhouse. Do you see the difficulty?

The problem is that we are always changing bodies, life after life. It is a serious problem. We have no fixed position; we do not know where we will be placed within the 8,400,000 species of life. But there is a solution: If somehow or other a person develops pure Kṛṣṇa consciousness, he will go to Kṛṣṇa at the time of death, and then he does not have to accept a material body again. He gets a spiritual body similar to Kṛṣṇa's, full of eternity, knowledge, and bliss.

Therefore we should take up the practice of Kṛṣṇa consciousness and execute it very seriously, without any deviation. We should not think that Kṛṣṇa consciousness is some kind of fashion. No, it is the most important function of every human being. Human life is simply meant for developing Kṛṣṇa consciousness. One has no other business.

Unfortunately, the people of the modern civilization have created so many other engagements that they are forgetting Kṛṣṇa consciousness. This is called *māyā,* or illusion. They are forgetting their real business. And the rascal, blind leaders are leading everyone to hell. They are simply *mis*leaders. People do not like to accept any authority. Still, they have accepted these rascals as leaders and are being misled. In this way both the rascal leaders and their unfortunate followers remain bound up by the stringent laws of material nature.

So, if somehow or other one comes in contact with Kṛṣṇa, one should seriously take up the process of Kṛṣṇa consciousness and catch hold of His lotus feet very tightly. If you hold on to Kṛṣṇa's lotus feet very tightly, *māyā* will not be able to harm you.

SPIRITUAL AND MATERIAL EDUCATION

The *Īśopaniṣad* states, "Those who are engaged in the culture of nescience shall enter into the darkest region of ignorance." There are two kinds of education, material and spiritual. Material education is called *jaḍa-vidyā. Jaḍa* means "that which cannot move," or matter. Spirit can move. Our body is a combination of spirit and matter. As long as the spirit is there, the body is moving. For example, a man's coat and pants move as long as the man wears them. It appears that the coat and pants are moving on their own, but actually it is the body that is moving them. Similarly, this body is moving because the spirit soul is moving it. Another example is the motorcar. The motorcar is moving because the driver is moving it. Only a fool thinks the motorcar is moving on its own. In spite of a wonderful mechanical arrangement, the motorcar cannot move on its own.

Since they are given only *jaḍa-vidyā,* a materialistic

education, people think that this material nature is working, moving, and manifesting so many wonderful things automatically. When we are at the seaside, we see the waves moving. But the waves are not moving automatically. The air is moving them. And something else is moving the air. In this way, if you go all the way back to the ultimate cause, you will find Kṛṣṇa, the cause of all causes. That is real education, to search out the ultimate cause.

So the *Īśopaniṣad* says that those who are captivated by the external movements of the material energy are worshiping nescience. In the modern civilization there are big, big institutions for understanding technology, how a motorcar or an airplane moves. They are studying how to manufacture so much machinery. But there is no educational institution for investigating how the spirit soul is moving. The actual mover is not being studied. Instead they are studying the external movements of matter.

When I lectured at the Massachusetts Institute of Technology, I asked the students, "Where is the technology to study the soul, the mover of the body?" They had no such technology. They could not answer satisfactorily because their education was simply *jaḍa-vidyā.* The *Īśopaniṣad* says that those who engage in the advancement of such materialistic education will go to the darkest region of existence. Therefore the present civilization is in a very dangerous position because there is no arrangement anywhere in the world for genuine spiritual education. In this way human society is being pushed to the darkest region of existence.

In a song, Śrīla Bhaktivinoda Ṭhākura has declared that materialistic education is simply an expansion of *māyā*. The more we advance in this materialistic education, the more our ability to understand God will be hampered. And at last we will declare, "God is dead." This is all ignorance and darkness.

So, the materialists are certainly being pushed into darkness. But there is another class—the so-called philosophers, mental speculators, religionists, and *yogīs*—who are going into still greater darkness because they are defying Kṛṣṇa. They are pretending to cultivate spiritual knowledge, but because they have no information of Kṛṣṇa, or God, their teachings are even more dangerous than those of the outright materialists. Why? Because they are misleading people into thinking they are giving real spiritual knowledge. The so-called *yoga* system they are teaching is misleading people: "Simply meditate, and you will understand that you are God." Kṛṣṇa never meditated to become God. He was God from His very birth. When He was a three-month-old baby, the Putanā demon attacked Him—and Kṛṣṇa sucked out her life air along with her breast milk. So Kṛṣṇa was God from the very beginning. That is God.

The nonsense so-called *yogīs* teach, "You become still and silent, and you will become God." How can I become silent? Is there any possibility of becoming silent? No, there is no such possibility. "Become desireless and you will become God." How can I become desireless? These are all bluffs. We cannot be desireless. We cannot be silent. But our desires and our activities can be purified. That is real knowledge. We should desire only to serve Kṛṣṇa. That is purification of desire. Instead of trying to be still and silent, we should dovetail our activities in Kṛṣṇa's service. As living entities, we have activities, desires, and a loving propensity, but they are being misdirected. If we direct them into Kṛṣṇa's service, that is the perfection of education.

We don't say that you should not become advanced in material education. You may, but at the same time you should become Kṛṣṇa conscious. That is our message. We don't say that you shouldn't manufacture motorcars. No. We say, "All right, you have manufactured these motorcars. Now employ them in Kṛṣṇa's service." That is our proposal.

So education is required, but if it is simply materialistic—if it is devoid of Kṛṣṇa consciousness—it is very, very dangerous. That is the teaching of the *Īśopaniṣad.*

KNOWLEDGE VS. NESCIENCE

The *Īśopaniṣad* says, "The wise have explained that one result is derived from the culture of knowledge and that a different result is obtained from the culture of nescience." As explained above, the real culture of knowledge is the advancement of spiritual knowledge. And advancement of knowledge in the matter of bodily comforts or to protect the body is the culture of nescience, because however you may try to protect this body, it will follow its natural course. What is that? Repeated birth and death, and while the body is manifested, disease and old age. People are very busy cultivating knowledge of this body, although they see that at every moment the body is decaying. The death of the body was fixed when it was born. That is a fact. So you cannot stop the natural course of this body—namely birth, old age, disease, and death.

The *Śrīmad-Bhāgavatam* (10.84.13) says that this body is nothing but a bag containing three primary elements—mucus, bile, and air—and that one who accepts this combination of mucus, bile, and air as himself is an ass. Even great philosophers and scientists take themselves to be this combination of mucus, bile, and air. This is their mistake. Actually, the philosophers and scientists are spirit souls, and according to their *karma* they are exhibiting their talent. They do not understand the law of *karma.*

Why do we find so many different personalities? If human beings are nothing but combinations of mucus, bile, and air, why are they not identical? One man is born a millionaire; another is unable to have two full meals a day, despite struggling very hard. Why this difference? Because of the law of *karma,* action and reaction. One who understands this mystery is in knowledge.

Human life is meant for understanding the mystery of life. And one who fails to utilize this human form for this purpose is a *kṛpana,* a miser. This is stated in the *Garga Upaniṣad.* If you get one million dollars and do not use it, thinking, "Oh, I will simply keep this bank balance of one million dollars," you are a *kṛpaṇa.* You do not know how to use your money. On the other hand, one who uses his million dollars to make another million dollars is intelligent. Similarly, this human body is invaluable. One who uses it for cultivating spiritual knowledge is a *brāhmaṇa,* a wise man, and one who cultivates materialistic knowledge is a *kṛpana,* a miser. That is the difference between *brāhmaṇa* and *kṛpaṇa.*

One who uses this body the way cats and dogs do—for sense gratification—is a miser. He does not know how to use his "million dollars." Therefore it is the duty of the father, the mother, the state, and the teachers to provide spiritual education for their dependents from the very beginning of their lives. Indeed, the *Śrīmad-Bhāgavatam* says that one should not become a father, a mother, a teacher, or a governmental head unless one is able to elevate one's dependents to the platform of spiritual knowledge, which can save them from repeated birth and death.

THE WAY OF KNOWING GOD

In the Vedic disciplic succession, the spiritual masters always base their statements on what they have heard from authoritative sources, never on personal experience. Trying to understand things by one's own direct experience is the material process of gaining knowledge, technically called *pratyakṣa.* The Vedic method is different. It is called *śruti,* which means "to hear from authoritative sources." That is the secret of Vedic understanding.

With your imperfect senses you should not try to understand things that are beyond your experimental powers. That is not possible. Suppose you want to know who your father is. Can you find out by experimenting?

Is it possible? No. Then how can you know who your father is? By hearing from the proper authority, your mother. This is common sense. And if you cannot know your material father by the experimental process, how can you know the Supreme Father by the experimental process? Kṛṣṇa is the original father. He is the father of the father of the father, all the way down to you. So if you cannot understand your immediate father, the previous generation, by the experimental process, how can you know God, or Kṛṣṇa, in this way?

People search for God by the experimental process, but after much searching they fail. Then they say, "Oh, there is no God. I am God." But the *Īśopaniṣad* says that one should try to learn about God not by the experimental process but by hearing. From whom should one hear? From a shopkeeper? From fanatics? No. One should hear from those who are *dhīra. Dhīra* means "one whose senses are not agitated by material influence."

There are different kinds of agitation—agitations of the mind, the power of speech, and anger, and agitations of the tongue, belly, and genitals. When we become angry, we forget everything and can do any nonsense and speak so much nonsense. For the agitation of the tongue there are so many advertisements: "Here is liquor, here is chicken, here is beef." Will we die without liquor, chicken, or beef? No. For the human beings Kṛṣṇa has given so many nice things to eat—grains, fruits, milk, and so on.

The cow produces milk abundantly, not for herself but for human beings. That is proper human food. God says, "Mrs. Cow, although you are producing milk, you cannot drink it. It is for the human beings, who are more advanced than animals." Of course, in the infant stage animals live off their mother's milk, so the calves drink some of the cow's milk. But the cow gives excess milk, and that excess is specifically meant for us.

We should accept whatever God has ordained as our proper food. But no, because of the agitation of the tongue, we think, "Why should I be satisfied eating grains, milk products, vegetables, and fruits? Let me maintain a slaughterhouse and kill these cows. After drinking their milk, just as I drank my mother's milk, let me kill them to satisfy my tongue." You shouldn't think such nonsense but should hear from the *dhīras,* or *svāmīs,* who have controlled their senses. A *svāmī,* or *gosvāmī,* is one who has control over the six agitations: the speech, the mind, anger, the tongue, the belly, and the genitals.

There is a nice poem by Kālidāsa called *Kumāra-sambhava* describing how Lord Śiva is *dhīra.* When Lord Śiva's wife, Satī, heard Śiva being blasphemed at a sacrifice performed by her father, she committed suicide. Upon hearing about his wife's suicide, Lord Śiva became very angry and left this planet to meditate elsewhere. During that time there was a war between the demons and the demigods. The demigods needed a good general. They concluded that if Lord Śiva were to beget a son, the son would be able to lead them in the fight against the demons. Lord Śiva was completely naked while meditating. So Pārvatī, the reincarnation of Satī, was sent to agitate his genitals for sex. But he was not agitated. He remained silent.

At this point Kālidāsa remarks, "Here is a *dhīra*. He is naked, and a young girl is touching his genitals, but still he is not agitated."

Dhīra means that even if there is some cause for agitation, one will not be agitated. If there is some very nice food, my tongue should not bc agitated to taste it. If there is a very nice girl or boy, still I should not be agitated sexually. In this way one who is *dhīra* is able to control the six agitating forces mentioned above. It is not that Lord Śiva was impotent: he was *dhīra*. Similarly, Kṛṣṇa danced with so many girls, but there was no sex appetite.

So, you have to hear from a person who is *dhīra*. If you hear from the *adhīra*, from those who are not self-controlled, then whatever knowledge you learn will be useless. In the *Īśopaniṣad,* a student has approached his spiritual master to inquire from him, and the spiritual master is saying, "This is what I have heard from authoritative sources." The spiritual master is not inventing something from his own experience. He is presenting exactly what he has heard.

So we have nothing to research. Everything is there. We simply have to hear from a person who is *dhīra,* who is not agitated by the six urges. That is the Vedic process of gaining knowledge. And if we try to use some other process, we will remain covered by nescience.

The *Īśopaniṣad* states, "Only one who can learn the process of nescience and that of transcendental knowledge side by side can transcend the influence of repeated birth and death and enjoy the full blessings of immortality." People do not understand what immortality is. They think it is a mythological idea. They are proud of their advancement of knowledge, but there are many things they do not know, nor can they ever know them by their modern system of experimentation.

So if you want real knowledge, you should take knowledge from the literature known as the *Vedas*. (The word *veda* means "knowledge.") Part of the *Vedas* are the 108 *Upaniṣads,* out of which eleven are very important. Of those eleven, the *Īśopaniṣad* stands first. In the word *upaniṣad, upa* means "near." So the knowledge in the *Īśopaniṣad* will take you nearer to Kṛṣṇa.

In learned society the *Vedas* are accepted as *śruti,* or primary evidence. The *Vedas* are not knowledge established by the research work of contaminated, conditioned souls. Such people have imperfect senses, and so they cannot see things as they are. They simply theorize, "It may be like this. It may be like that." That is not knowledge. Knowledge is definite, without any doubt or mistake. Conditioned souls commit mistakes, become illusioned, and cheat. How do they cheat? When one who does not understand the *Bhagavad-gītā* writes a commentary on it, he is cheating the innocent public. Someone has a title as a scholar, so he takes advantage of the popularity of the *Bhagavad-gītā* and writes a commentary. Such so-called scholars claim that anyone can give his own opinion. But in the *Bhagavad-gītā* Kṛṣṇa says that only His devotee can understand the *Gītā.* So these so-called scholars are cheating.

The conclusion is that if you want genuine spiritual knowledge you have to approach a bona fide spiritual master who has realized the Absolute Truth. Otherwise you will remain in darkness. You cannot think, "Oh, I may or may not accept a spiritual master. In any case, there are books that I can learn from." No, the Vedic injunction is *tad-vijñānārthaṁ sa gurum evābhigacchet.* The word *gacchet* means "one must go," not that one may or may not go. To understand transcendental knowledge, one *must* go to a spiritual master. That is the Vedic injunction.

You must know two things: what is *māyā* (illusion) and what is Kṛṣṇa. Then your knowledge is perfect. Of course, Kṛṣṇa is so nice that if you somehow or other fully surrender to Him, all your searching for knowledge will be finished: not only will you know what Kṛṣṇa is, but you will automatically learn what *māyā* is. Kṛṣṇa will give you intelligence from within.

So, by the mercy of both the spiritual master and Kṛṣṇa, one takes up devotional service. How is that? Their mercy runs on parallel lines. If you have not yet found a spiritual master but are sincere, Kṛṣṇa will direct you to a bona fide spiritual master. And if you get a bona fide spiritual master, he will take you to Kṛṣṇa. Kṛṣṇa is always sitting in your heart as the *caitya-guru,* the spiritual master within. It is that *caitya-guru* who manifests Himself externally as the spiritual master. Therefore the spiritual master is the direct representative of Kṛṣṇa.

The *Īśopaniṣad* says we should learn what *vidyā* and *avidyā* are. *Avidyā* is ignorance under the guise of materialistic knowledge. Śrīla Bhaktivinoda Ṭhākura writes in one of his songs that "advancement of material knowledge is simply the advancement of *māyā's* jurisdiction." The more you become implicated in material knowledge, the less you can understand Kṛṣṇa consciousness. Those who are advanced in material knowledge think, "What use is this Kṛṣṇa consciousness movement?" They have no attraction for spiritual knowledge; they are too absorbed in *avidyā.*

Some Indian boys reject the spiritual culture of India and come to the West to learn technology. When they see that I have introduced in the West the things they rejected in India, they are surprised. One reason I came to the West is that modern India has rejected spiritual knowledge. Today Indians think that if they can imitate Western technology, they will be happy. This is *māyā.* They do not see that those who are three hundred times more technologically advanced than the Indians are not happy. India will not be able to equal American or European technology for at least three hundred years because the Western countries have been developing technology for a very long time. But since the time of creation Indian culture has been a spiritual culture.

Vidyā, or genuine spiritual knowledge, does not depend on technology. Śrīla Vyāsadeva is the original *guru* of Vedic knowledge. How was he living? In a cottage in Baḍarikāśrama. But just see his knowledge! He wrote so many *Purāṇas,* including the *Śrīmad-Bhāgavatam*. He also wrote the *Vedānta-sūtra* and the *Mahābhārata*. If you studied every single verse written by Vyāsadeva, it would take your whole life. The *Śrīmad-Bhāgavatam* alone has no less than eighteen thousand verses. And each verse is so full of meaning that it would take a whole lifetime to fully understand it. This is Vedic culture.

There is no knowledge comparable to that contained in the Vedic literature—not only spiritual knowledge, but material knowledge also. The *Vedas* discuss astronomy, mathematics, and many other subjects. It is not that in ancient times there were no airplanes. They are mentioned in the *Purāṇas.* These airplanes were so strong and swift that they could easily reach other planets. It is not that there was no advancement of material knowledge in the Vedic age. It was there. But the people then did not consider it so important. They were interested in spiritual knowledge.

So, one should know what knowledge is, and what nescience is. If we advance in nescience, or material knowledge, we will have to undergo repeated birth and death. Moreover, there is no guarantee what your next birth will be. That is not in your hands. Now you are happy being an American, but after quitting this body you cannot dictate, "Please give me an American body again." Yes, you may get an American body, but it may be an American cow's body. Then you are destined for the slaughterhouse.

So, cultivating material knowledge—nationalism, socialism, this "ism," that "ism"—is simply a dangerous waste of time. Better to cultivate real knowledge, Vedic knowledge, which leads one to surrender to Kṛṣṇa. As Kṛṣṇa says in the *Bhagavad-gītā* (7.19), *bahūnāṁ janmanām ante jñānavān māṁ prapadyate.* After many, many births, one who is in genuine knowledge comes to Kṛṣṇa and surrenders to Him, realizing, "O Kṛṣṇa, You are everything." This is the culmination of all cultivation of knowledge.

BEYOND THE WHITE LIGHT OF BRAHMAN

The *Īśopaniṣad* states, "One should know perfectly the Personality of Godhead and His transcendental name, as well as the temporary material creation with its temporary demigods, men, and animals. When one knows these, he surpasses death and the ephemeral cosmic manifestation with it, and in the eternal kingdom of God he enjoys his eternal life of bliss and knowledge. O my Lord, sustainer of all that lives, Your real face is covered by Your dazzling effulgence. Kindly remove that covering and exhibit Yourself to Your pure devotee."

Here the *Īśopaniṣad* mentions the kingdom of God. Every planet, both spiritual and material, has a predominating deity. In the sun, for example, the predominating deity is Vivasvān. We get this information from the *Bhagavad-gītā*. So, there are millions and trillions of universes within the material sky, and within each universe are millions and trillions of planets, and in every planet there is a predominating deity.

Beyond the material sky is the *brahmajyoti,* or spiritual sky, where there are innumerable Vaikuṇṭha planets. Each Vaikuṇṭha planet is predominated by the Supreme Lord in His Nārāyaṇa form, and each Nārāyaṇa has a different name—Pradyumna, Aniruddha, Saṅkarṣaṇa, etc. One cannot see these planets because they are covered by the spiritual *brahmajyoti* effulgence, just as one cannot see the sun globe on account of the dazzling sunshine. The effulgence in the spiritual sky is coming out of Kṛṣṇa's planet, Goloka

Vṛndāvana, which is above even Vaikuṇṭha and where Kṛṣṇa alone is the predominator.

The planet of the Absolute Truth, Kṛṣṇa, is covered by the Brahman effulgence. One has to penetrate that effulgence in order to see the Lord. Therefore in the *Īśopaniṣad* the devotee prays, "Kindly remove Your effulgence so I can see You." The Māyāvādī philosophers do not know that there is something beyond the *brahmajyoti.* But here in the *Īśopaniṣad* is the Vedic evidence that the *brahmajyoti* is simply a golden effulgence covering the real face of the Supreme Lord.

The idea is that Kṛṣṇa's planet and the Vaikuṇṭha planets are beyond the Brahman effulgence and that only devotees can enter those spiritual planets. The *jñānīs,* the mental speculators, practice severe austerities to enter the Brahman effulgence. But the demons who are killed by Kṛṣṇa are immediately transferred to that Brahman effulgence. So just consider: Is the place that is given to the enemies of Kṛṣṇa very covetable? If my enemy comes to my house, I may give him some place to stay, but if my intimate friend comes, I give him a much nicer place to stay. So this Brahman effulgence is not at all covetable.

Śrīla Prabodhānanda Sarasvatī has composed a nice verse in which he says that for the devotee, for one who has attained the mercy of the Lord, the Brahman effulgence is just like hell. Then what about heaven? The *karmīs,* or fruitive workers, are very eager to go to the heavenly planets, where the demigods reside. But for the devotees heaven is just a will-o'-the-wisp. They are not at all attracted to go there. And then there are the mystic *yogīs,* who try very strenuously to control the senses in order to attain special powers. The senses are like venomous serpents because as soon as you indulge in sense gratification—as soon as the senses "bite" you—you become degraded. But the devotee says, "I do not fear the poisonous serpents of the senses." Why? "Because I have extracted their fangs." In other words, by engaging his senses in Kṛṣṇa's service, the devotee is no longer tempted to indulge in sense gratification, and thus his senses cannot drag him down to a hellish condition of life.

In this way, the devotees are above the *karmīs, jñānīs,* and *yogīs.* The devotees' place is the highest because only by devotion can one understand God. Kṛṣṇa does not say you can understand Him by fruitive work. He does not say you can understand Him by speculation. He does not say you can understand Him by mystic *yoga*. He clearly says (Bg. 18.55), *bhaktyā mām abhijānāti yāvān yaś cāsmi tattvataḥ:* "Only by devotional service can one truly understand Me as I am."

Except for devotional service, there is no possibility of understanding the Absolute Truth. Any other process is imperfect because it is based on speculation. For example, the scientists may speculate on what the sun planet is, but because they have no access there, they cannot actually know what the sun planet is. They can only speculate. That's all. Once three blind men came upon an elephant. They began feeling the elephant and speculating on what it was. One felt its big legs and concluded, "Oh, the elephant is just like a pillar." The second man felt the trunk and concluded, "Oh, this elephant is just like a snake." And the third man felt the belly of the elephant and concluded, "This elephant is like a big boat." But actually, the blind men did not know what the elephant really was.

If you have no ability to see something, you can only speculate about it. Therefore the *Īśopaniṣad* says, "Please remove this brilliant effulgence covering Your face so I can see You." That seeing power is bestowed upon the devotee by Kṛṣṇa when He sees the devotee's love for Him. As the *Brahma-saṁhitā* says, *premāñjana-cchurita-bhakti-vilocanena:* The devotees anoint their eyes with the salve of love of God, and therefore they can see the Lord's beautiful form within their hearts. In India there is a special eye ointment. If you apply it you can immediately see clearly. Similarly, if you smear your eyes with the ointment of love of Godhead, you will see God always. This is the way of understanding God—by service and by enhancing your love for Him. This love can be developed only by devotional service; otherwise there is no possibility of achieving it. So the more you increase your spirit of service to God, the more you increase your dormant love for God. And as soon as you are in the perfectional stage of love of God, you will see God always, at every moment.

His Divine Grace
A. C. Bhaktivedanta Swami Prabhupāda
Founder-Ācārya of the International Society for Krishna Consciousness

PLATE ONE: Lord Caitanya and His associates propagated the congregational chanting of the Lord's holy names, the best way to achieve peace, both individually and worldwide. *From left:* Śrī Advaitācārya, Lord Nityānanda, Lord Caitanya, Śrī Gadādhara, and Śrīvāsa Ṭhākura. (*p. 80*)

PLATE TWO: Lord Kṛṣṇa enjoys loving exchanges with all living creatures in Goloka Vṛndāvana, His eternal spiritual abode. (*p. 21*)

PLATE THREE: According to the strict laws of *karma* and reincarnation, one who likes to expose his or her body and engage in unrestricted sex may have to stand naked for hundreds of years as a tree, one who is lazy and likes to sleep too much risks becoming a bear and having

to hibernate for months every year, one who is a rabid meat-eater may become a tiger in his next life, and one who eats abominable foods risks becoming a stool-eating hog in his next life. (*p. 3*)

PLATE FOUR: Without Kṛṣṇa consciousness, human life is nothing more than polished animal life. We may eat in an expensive restaurant, sleep in a luxurious hotel, raise a family in the suburbs, and

defend ourselves with modern weapons, but these activities are essentially the same eating, sleeping, mating, and defending that go on in every species of life. (*p. 59*)

PLATE FIVE: Attachment to family, home, etc., securely traps the materialist in the jungle of household life, where he is victimized by those he works so hard to please. (*pp. 57–62*)

CHAPTER 2

BAD KARMA

The Śrīmad-Bhāgavatam is an ancient Sanskrit scripture that contains the essence of all Vedic wisdom, recording the teachings of the Lord's devotees, as well as those of the Lord in many of His incarnations. In this Thirtieth Chapter of the Third Canto, an incarnation of Kṛṣṇa's named Kapiladeva graphically describes the results of sin. Śrīla Prabhupāda explains the texts in his purports.

TEXT 1: The Personality of Godhead said, "As a mass of clouds does not know the powerful influence of the wind, a person engaged in material consciousness does not know the powerful strength of the time factor, by which he is being carried."

PURPORT: The great politician-*paṇḍita* named Cāṇakya said that even one moment of time cannot be returned, even if one is prepared to pay millions of dollars. One cannot calculate the amount of loss there is in wasting valuable time. Whether materially or spiritually, one should be very alert in utilizing the time which he has at his disposal. A conditioned soul lives in a particular body for a fixed measurement of time, and it is recommended in the scriptures that within that small measurement of time one has to finish Kṛṣṇa consciousness and thus gain release from the influence of the time factor. But, unfortunately, those who are not in Kṛṣṇa consciousness are carried away by the strong power of time without their knowledge, as clouds are carried by the wind.

TEXT 2: "Whatever is produced by the materialist with great pain and labor for so-called happiness, the Supreme Personality, as the time factor, destroys, and for this reason the conditioned soul laments."

PURPORT: The main function of the time factor, which is a representative of the Supreme Personality of Godhead, is to destroy everything. The materialists, in material consciousness, are engaged in producing so many things in the name of economic development. They think that by advancing in satisfying the material needs of man they will be happy, but they forget that everything they have produced will be destroyed in due course of time. From history we can see that there were many powerful empires on the surface of the globe that were constructed with great pain and great perseverance, but in due course of time they have all been destroyed. Still the foolish materialists cannot understand that they are simply wasting time in producing so-called material necessities, which are destined to be vanquished in due course of time. This waste of energy is due to the ignorance of the mass of people, who do not know that they are eternal and that they have an eternal engagement also. They do not know that this span of life in a particular type of body is but a flash in the eternal journey. Not knowing this fact, they take the small flash of their present life to be everything, and they waste time in improving economic conditions.

TEXT 3: "The misguided materialist does not know that his very body is impermanent and that the attractions of home, land, and wealth, which are in relationship to that body, are also temporary. Out of ignorance only, he thinks that everything is permanent."

PURPORT: The materialist thinks that persons engaged in Kṛṣṇa consciousness are crazy fellows wasting time by chanting Hare Kṛṣṇa, but actually he does not know that he himself is in the darkest region of craziness because of accepting his body as permanent. And in relation to his body he accepts his home, his country, his society, and all other paraphernalia as permanent. This materialistic acceptance of the permanence of home, land, etc. is called the illusion of *māyā*. This is clearly mentioned here. *Mohād gṛha-kṣetra-vasūni:* out of illusion only does the materialist accept his home, his land, and his money as permanent. Out of this illusion have grown family life, national life, and economic development, which are very important factors in modern civilization. A Kṛṣṇa conscious person knows that this economic development of human society is but temporary illusion.

In another part of the *Śrīmad-Bhāgavatam,* the acceptance of the body as oneself, the acceptance of others as kinsmen in relationship to one's body, and the acceptance of the land of one's birth as worshipable are declared to be the products of an animal civilization. When, however, one is enlightened in Kṛṣṇa consciousness, one can use these for the service of the Lord. That is a very suitable proposition. Everything has a relationship with Kṛṣṇa. When all economic development and material advancement are utilized to advance the cause of Kṛṣṇa consciousness, a new phase of progressive life arises.

TEXT 4: "In whatever species of life the living entity appears, he finds a particular type of satisfaction in that species, and he is never averse to being situated in such a condition."

PURPORT: The satisfaction of the living entity in a particular type of body, even if it is most abominable, is called illusion. A man in a higher position may feel dissatisfaction with the standard of life of a lower-grade man, but the lower-grade man is satisfied in that position because of the spell of *māyā,* the external energy. *Māyā* has two phases of activity. One is called *prakṣepātmikā,* and the other is called *āvaraṇātmikā. Āvaraṇātmikā* means "covering," and *prakṣepātmikā* means "pulling down." In any condition of life, the materialistic person or animal will be satisfied because his knowledge is covered by the influence of *māyā*. In the lower grade or lower species of life, the development of consciousness is so poor that one cannot understand whether one is happy or distressed. This is called *āvaraṇātmikā*. Even a hog, who lives by eating stool, thinks himself happy, although a person in a higher mode of life sees how abominable that life is.

TEXT 5: "While deluded by the covering influence of the illusory energy, the living entity feels little inclined to cast off his body, even when in hell, for he takes delight in hellish enjoyment."

PURPORT: It is said that once Indra, the king of heaven, was cursed by his spiritual master, Bṛhaspati, on account of his misbehavior, and he became a hog on this planet. After many days, when Brahmā wanted to recall him to his heavenly kingdom, Indra, in the form of a hog, forgot everything of his royal position in the heavenly kingdom, and he refused to go back. This is the spell of *māyā*. Even Indra forgets his heavenly standard of life and is satisfied with the standard of a hog's life.

By the influence of *māyā* the conditioned soul becomes so affectionate toward his particular type of body that even if someone says to him, "Give up this body, and immediately you will have a king's body," he will not agree. This attachment strongly affects all conditioned living entities. Lord Kṛṣṇa personally canvasses, "Give up everything in this material world.

Come to Me, and I shall give you all protection," but we are not agreeable. We think, "We are quite all right. Why should we surrender unto Kṛṣṇa and go back to His kingdom?" This is called illusion, or *māyā*. Everyone is satisfied with his standard of living, however abominable it may be.

TEXT 6: "Such satisfaction with one's standard of living is due to deep-rooted attraction for body, wife, home, children, animals, wealth, and friends. In such association, the conditioned soul thinks himself quite perfect."

PURPORT: This so-called perfection of human life is a concoction. Therefore it is said that however materially qualified a person may be, if he is not a devotee of the Lord he has no good qualities because he is hovering on the mental plane, which will drag him again to the material existence of temporary life. One who acts on the mental plane cannot get promotion to the spiritual plane. Such a person is always sure to glide down again to material life. Still, in the association of so-called society, friendship, and love, the conditioned soul feels completely satisfied.

TEXT 7: "Although he is always burning with anxiety, such a fool always performs all kinds of mischievous activities with the unfulfillable hope of maintaining his so-called family and society."

PURPORT: It is said that it is easier to maintain a great empire than a small family, especially in these days, when the influence of Kali-yuga is so strong that everyone is harassed and full of anxieties because of accepting the false presentation of *māyā's* family. The family we maintain is created by *māyā;* it is the perverted reflection of the family in Kṛṣṇaloka. In Kṛṣṇaloka there are also family, friends, society, father, and mother; everything is there, but they are eternal. Here, as we change bodies our family relationships also change. Sometimes we are in a family of human beings, sometimes in a family of demigods, sometimes a family of cats or dogs.

Family, society, and friendship are flickering, and so they are called *asat.* It is said that as long as we are attached to this *asat*—this temporary, nonexistent society and family—we are always full of anxieties. The materialists do not know that the family, society, and friendship here in this material world are only shadows, and thus they become attached. Naturally their hearts are always burning, but in spite of all inconvenience, they still work to maintain such false families because they have no information of the real family association with Kṛṣṇa.

TEXT 8: "He gives heart and senses to a woman, who falsely charms him with *māyā.* He enjoys solitary embraces and talking with her, and he is enchanted by the sweet words of the small children."

PURPORT: Family life within the kingdom of the illusory energy, *māyā,* is just like a prison for the eternal living entity. In prison a prisoner is shackled by iron chains and iron bars. Similarly, a conditioned soul is shackled by the charming beauty of a woman, by her solitary embraces and talks of so-called love, and by the sweet words of his small children. Thus he forgets his real identity.

In this verse the words *strīṇām asatīnām* indicate that womanly love exists just to agitate the mind of man. Actually, in the material world there is no love. Both the woman and the man are interested in their sense gratification. For sense gratification a woman creates an illusory love, and the man becomes enchanted by such false love and forgets his real duty. When there are children as the result of such a combination, the next attraction is to the sweet words of the children. The love of the woman at home and the talk of the children make one a secure prisoner, and thus he cannot leave his home. Such a person is termed, in Vedic language, a *gṛhamedhī,* which means "one whose center of attraction is home." The word *gṛhastha* refers to one who lives with family, wife, and children but whose real purpose of living is to develop Kṛṣṇa consciousness. One is therefore advised to become a *gṛhastha,* not a *gṛhamedhī.* The *gṛhastha's* concern is to get out of the family life created by illusion and enter into real family life with Kṛṣṇa, whereas the *gṛhamedhī's* business is to repeatedly chain himself to so-called family life, in one life after another, and perpetually remain in the darkness of *māyā.*

TEXT 9: "The attached householder remains in his family life, which is full of diplomacy and politics. Always spreading miseries and controlled by acts of sense gratification, he acts just to counteract the reactions of all his miseries, and if he can successfully counteract such miseries, he thinks he is happy."

PURPORT: In the *Bhagavad-gītā* the Personality of Godhead Himself certifies the material world as an impermanent place that is full of miseries. There is no question of happiness in this material world, either individually or in terms of family, society, or country. If something is going on in the name of happiness, that is illusion. Here in this material world, happiness means successful counteraction of distress. The material world is so made that unless one becomes a clever diplomat, his life will be a failure. What to speak of human society, even in the society of lower animals, the birds and beasts cleverly manage their bodily demands of eating, sleeping, mating, and defending. Human society competes nationally or individually, and in the attempt to be successful the entire human society becomes full of diplomacy. We should always remember that in spite of all diplomacy and all intelligence in the struggle for existence, everything will end in a second by the supreme will. Therefore, all our attempts to become happy in this material world are simply a delusion offered by *māyā.*

TEXT 10: "He secures money by committing violence here and there, and although he employs it in the service of his family, he himself eats only a little portion of the food thus purchased, and he goes to hell for those for whom he earned the money in such an irregular way."

PURPORT: There is a Bengali proverb: "The person for whom I have stolen accuses me of being a thief." The family members for whom an attached person acts in so many criminal ways are never satisfied. In illusion an attached person serves such family members, and by serving them he is destined to enter into a hellish condition of life. For example, a thief steals something to maintain his family, and he is caught and imprisoned. This is the sum and substance of material existence and attachment to material society, friendship, and love. Although an attached family man is always engaged in getting money by hook or by crook for the maintenance of his family, he cannot enjoy more than what he could consume even without such criminal activities. A man who eats eight ounces of food may have to maintain a big family and earn money by any means to support that family, but he himself is not offered more than what he can eat, and sometimes he eats the remnants that are left after his family members are fed. Even by earning money by unfair means, he cannot enjoy life for himself. That is called the covering illusion of *māyā.*

The process of illusory service to society, country, and community is exactly the same everywhere; the same principle is applicable even to big national leaders. A national leader who is very great in serving his country is sometimes killed by his countrymen because of irregular service. In other words, one cannot satisfy his dependents by this illusory service, although one cannot get out of the service because being a servant is his constitutional position.

A living entity is constitutionally part and parcel of the Supreme Being, but he forgets that he has to render service to the Supreme Being and diverts his attention to serving others; this is called *māyā.* By serving others he falsely thinks that he is master. The head of a family thinks of himself as the master of the family, or the leader of a nation thinks of himself as the master of the nation, whereas actually he is serving, and by serving *māyā* he is gradually going to hell. Therefore a sane man should come to the point of Kṛṣṇa consciousness and engage in the service of the Supreme Lord, applying his whole life, all of his wealth, his entire intelligence, and his full power of speaking.

TEXTS 11–13: "When he suffers reverses in his occupation, he tries again and again to improve himself, but when he is baffled in all attempts and is ruined, he accepts money from others because of excessive greed. Thus the unfortunate man, unsuccessful in maintaining his family members, is bereft of all beauty. He always thinks of his failure, grieving very deeply. Seeing him unable to support them, his wife and others do not treat him with the same respect as before, even as miserly farmers do not accord the same treatment to their old and worn-out oxen."

PURPORT: Not only in the present age but from time immemorial no one has liked an old man who is unable to earn in the family. Even in the modern age, in some communities or states, the old men are given poison so that they will die as soon as possible. In some cannibalistic communities, the old grandfather is sportingly killed, and a feast is held in which his body is eaten. Here the example is given that a farmer does not like an old ox who has ceased to work. Similarly, when an attached person in family life becomes old and is unable to earn, he is no longer liked by his wife, sons, daughters, and other kinsmen, and he is consequently neglected, what to speak of not being given respect. It is judicious, therefore, to give up family attachment before one attains old age and take shelter of the Supreme Personality of Godhead. A person should employ himself in the Lord's service so that the Supreme Lord can take charge of him and he will not be neglected by his so-called kinsmen.

TEXT 14: "The foolish family man does not become averse to family life although he is maintained by those whom he once maintained. Deformed by the influence of old age, he prepares himself to meet ultimate death."

PURPORT: Family attraction is so strong that even if a person is neglected by family members in his old age, he cannot give up family affection, and he remains at home just like a dog. In the Vedic way of life, it is advised that before getting too weak and being baffled in material activities, and before becoming diseased, one should give up family life and engage oneself completely in the service of the Lord for the remaining days of his life.

Therefore the Vedic scriptures enjoin that as soon as one passes fifty years of age, he must give up family life and live alone in the forest. After preparing himself fully, he should become a *sannyāsī,* travel widely, and distribute the knowledge of spiritual life to each and every home.

TEXT 15: "Thus he remains at home just like a pet dog and eats whatever is so negligently given to him. Afflicted with many illnesses, such as dyspepsia and loss of appetite, he eats only very small morsels of food, and he becomes an invalid, who cannot work any more."

PURPORT: Before meeting death a man is sure to become a diseased invalid, and when he is neglected by his family members, his life becomes less than a dog's because he is put into so many miserable conditions. Vedic literatures enjoin, therefore, that before the arrival of such miserable conditions, a man should leave home and die without the knowledge of his family members. If a man leaves home and dies without his family's knowing, that is considered a glorious death. But an attached family man wants his family members to carry him in a great procession even after his death, and although he will not be able to see how the procession goes, he still desires that his body be taken gorgeously in procession. Thus he is happy without even knowing where he has to go when he leaves his body for the next life.

TEXTS 16–17: "In that diseased condition, a man's eyes bulge due to the pressure of air from within, and his glands become congested with mucus. He has difficulty breathing, and upon exhaling and inhaling he produces a sound like *ghura-ghura,* a rattling within the throat. In this way he comes under the clutches of death and lies down, surrounded by lamenting friends and relatives, and although he wants to speak with them, he no longer can because he is under the control of time."

PURPORT: For formality's sake, when a man is lying on his deathbed, his relatives come to him, and sometimes they cry very loudly, addressing the dying man: "O my father!" "O my friend!" or "O my husband!" In that pitiable condition the dying man wants to speak with them and instruct them of his desires, but because he is fully under the control of the time factor, death, he cannot express himself, and that causes him inconceivable pain. He is already in a painful condition because of disease, and his glands and throat are choked up with mucus. He is already in a very difficult position, and when he is addressed by his relatives in that way, his grief increases.

TEXT 18: "Thus the man who engaged with uncontrolled senses in maintaining his family dies in great grief, seeing his relatives crying. He dies most pathetically, in great pain and without consciousness."

PURPORT: In the *Bhagavad-gītā* it is said that at the time of death one will be absorbed in the thoughts he cultivated during his lifetime. A person who had no idea other than to properly maintain his family members must have family affairs in his last thoughts. That is the natural sequence for a common man. The common man does not know the destiny of his life; he is simply busy in this present flash of life, maintaining his family. At the last stage, no one is satisfied with how he has improved the family economic condition; everyone thinks that he could not provide sufficiently. Because of his deep family affection, he forgets his main duty of controlling his senses and improving his spiritual consciousness. Sometimes a dying man entrusts the family affairs to either his son or some relative, saying, "I am going. Please look after the family." He does not know where he is going, but even at the time of death he is anxious about how his family will be maintained. Sometimes it is seen that a dying man requests the physician to increase his life at least for a few years so that the family maintenance plan which he has begun can be completed. These are the material diseases of the conditioned soul. He completely forgets his real engagement—to become Kṛṣṇa conscious—and is always serious about planning to maintain his family, although he changes families one after another.

TEXT 19: "At death, he sees the messengers of the lord of death come before him, their eyes full of wrath, and in great fear he passes stool and urine."

PURPORT: There are two kinds of transmigration of a living entity after passing away from the present body. One kind of transmigration is to go to the controller of sinful activities, who is known as Yamarāja, and the other is to go to the higher planets, up to Vaikuṇṭha. Here Lord Kapila describes how persons engaged in activities of sense gratification to maintain a family are treated by the messengers of Yamarāja, called Yamadūtas. At the time of death the Yamadūtas become the custodians of those persons who have strongly gratified their senses. They take charge of the dying man and take him to the planet where Yamarāja resides. The conditions there are described in the following verses.

TEXT 20: "As a criminal is arrested for punishment by the constables of the state, a person engaged in criminal sense gratification is similarly arrested by the Yamadūtas, who bind him by the neck with strong rope and cover his subtle body so that he may undergo severe punishment."

PURPORT: Every living entity is covered by a subtle body and a gross body. The subtle body is the covering of mind, ego, intelligence, and consciousness. It is said in the scriptures that the constables of Yamarāja cover the subtle body of the culprit and take him to the abode of Yamarāja to be punished in a way that he is able to tolerate. He does not die from this punishment because if he died, then who would suffer the punishment? It is not the business of the constables of Yamarāja to put one to death. In fact, it is not possible to kill a living entity because factually he is eternal; he simply has to suffer the consequences of his activities of sense gratification.

The process of punishment is explained in the *Caitanya-caritāmṛta.* Formerly the king's men would take a criminal in a boat in the middle of the river. They would dunk him by grasping a bunch of his hair and thrusting him completely under water, and when he was almost suffocated, the king's constables would take him out of the water and allow him to breathe for some time, and then they would again dunk him in the water to suffocate. This sort of punishment is inflicted upon the forgotten soul by Yamarāja, as will be described in the following verses.

TEXT 21: "While carried by the constables of Yamarāja, he is overwhelmed and trembles in their hands. While passing on the road he is bitten by dogs, and he can remember the sinful activities of his life. He is thus terribly distressed."

PURPORT: It appears from this verse that while passing from this planet to the planet of Yamarāja, the culprit arrested by Yamarāja's constables meets many dogs, which bark and bite just to remind him of his criminal activities of sense gratification. It is said in the *Bhagavad-gītā* that one becomes almost blind and is bereft of all sense when he is infuriated by the desire for sense gratification. He forgets everything. A man is bereft of all intelligence when he is too attracted by sense gratification, and he forgets that he has to suffer the consequences also. Here the chance for recounting his activities of sense gratification is given by the dogs engaged by Yamarāja. While we live in the gross body, such activities of sense gratification are encouraged, even by modern governments. In many states all over the world, the government encourages such activities by pushing birth control. Women are supplied pills, and they are allowed to go to a clinical laboratory to get assistance for abortions. This is going on as a result of sense gratification. Actually sex is meant for begetting a good child, but because people have no control over the senses and there is no institution to train them to control the senses, the poor people fall victim to the criminal offenses of sense gratification, and they are punished after death as described in these passages of the *Śrīmad-Bhāgavatam.*

TEXTS 22–24: "Under the scorching sun, the criminal has to pass through roads of hot sand with forest fires on both sides. He is whipped on the back by the constables because of his inability to walk, and he is afflicted by hunger and thirst. But unfortunately there is no drinking water, no shelter, and no place for rest on the road. While passing on that road to the abode of Yamarāja, he falls down in fatigue, and sometimes he becomes unconscious, but he is forced to rise again.

"In this way he is very quickly brought to the presence of Yamarāja. Thus he has to pass ninety-nine thousand *yojanas* within two or three moments, and then he is at once engaged in the torturous punishment he is destined to suffer."

PURPORT: One *yojana* is eight miles, and thus he has to pass along a road that is as much as 792,000 miles long. Such a long distance is passed over within a few moments only. The subtle body is covered by the constables so that the living entity can travel such a long distance quickly and at the same time tolerate the suffering. This covering, although material, is of such fine elements that material scientists cannot discover what the coverings are made of. To pass 792,000 miles within a few moments seems wonderful to the modern space travelers. They have so far traveled at a speed of 18,000 miles per hour, but here we see that a criminal passes 792,000 miles within a few seconds only, although the process is not spiritual but material.

TEXT 25: "He is placed in the midst of burning pieces of wood, and his limbs are set on fire. In some cases he is made to eat his own flesh or have it eaten by others."

PURPORT: This verse and the next three verses describe the sinful living entity's punishment. The first description is that the criminal has to eat his own flesh, burning with fire, or allow others like himself who are present there to eat it. In the last great war, people in concentration camps sometimes ate their own stool, so there is no wonder that in Yamasādana, the abode of Yamarāja, a meat-eater who had a very enjoyable life eating others' flesh has to eat his own flesh.

TEXTS 26–28: "His entrails are pulled out by the hounds and vultures of hell, even though he is still alive to see it, and he is subjected to torment by serpents, scorpions, gnats, and other creatures that bite him. Next his limbs are lopped off and torn asunder by elephants. He is hurled down from hilltops, and he is also held captive either in water or in a cave.

"Men and women whose lives were built upon indulgence in illicit sex are put into many kinds of miserable conditions in the hells known as Tāmisra, Andhatāmisra, and Raurava."

PURPORT: The lives of all materialistic people, who are undergoing severe tribulation in the struggle for existence, are based on sex. Therefore, in the Vedic civilization sex is allowed only in a restricted way; it is for the married couple, and only for begetting children. But when sex is indulged in for sense gratification illegally and illicitly, both the man and the woman await severe punishment in this world or after death. In this world they are punished by virulent diseases like syphilis and gonorrhea, and in the next life, as we see in this passage of the *Śrīmad-Bhāgavatam,* they are put into various kinds of hellish conditions to suffer.

In the *Bhagavad-gītā,* First Chapter, illicit sex is also very much condemned, and it is said that one who produces children by illicit sex is sent to hell. It is confirmed here in the *Bhāgavatam* that such offenders are put into hellish conditions of life in Tāmisra, Andhatāmisra, and Raurava.

TEXT 29: Lord Kapila continued, "My dear mother, it is sometimes said that we experience hell or heaven on this planet, for hellish punishments are sometimes visible on this planet also."

PURPORT: Sometimes unbelievers do not accept these statements of scripture regarding hell. Lord Kapila therefore confirms them by saying that these hellish conditions are also visible on this planet. It is not that they are only on the planet where Yamarāja lives. On the planet of Yamarāja, the sinful man is given the chance to practice living in the hellish conditions that he will have to endure in the next life, and then he is given a chance to take birth on another planet to continue his hellish life.

For example, if a man is to be punished to remain in hell and eat stool and urine, then first of all he practices such habits on the planet of Yamarāja, and then he is given a particular type of body, that of a hog, so that he can eat stool and think he is enjoying life. It is stated previously that in any hellish condition, the conditioned soul thinks he is happy. Otherwise, it would not be possible for him to suffer hellish life.

TEXT 30: "After leaving this body, the man who maintained himself and his family members by sinful activities suffers a hellish life, and his relatives suffer also."

PURPORT: The mistake of modern civilization is that man does not believe in the next life. But whether he believes or not, the next life is there, and one has to suffer if one does not lead a responsible life in terms of the injunctions of authoritative scriptures like the *Vedas* and *Purāṇas.* Species lower than human beings are not responsible for their actions because they are made to act in a certain way, but in the developed life of human consciousness, one who does not act responsibly is sure to get a hellish life, as described herein.

TEXT 31: "He goes alone to the darkest regions of hell after quitting the present body, and the money he acquired by envying other living entities is the passage money with which he leaves this world."

PURPORT: When a man earns money by unfair means and maintains his family and himself with that money, the money is enjoyed by many members of the family, but he alone goes to hell and suffers the resultant sinful reactions accrued from such a violent and illicit life. For example, if a man secures some money by killing someone and with that money maintains his family, those who enjoy the black money earned by him are also partially responsible and are also sent to hell, but he who is the leader is especially punished. The money he earned is left in this world, and he takes only the sinful reaction.

In this world also, if a person acquires some money by murdering someone, the family is not hanged, although its members are sinfully contaminated. But the man who commits the murder and maintains his family is himself hanged as a murderer. The direct offender is more responsible for sinful activities than the indirect enjoyer. The great learned scholar Cāṇakya Paṇḍita says, therefore, that whatever one has in his possession had better be spent for the cause of *sat,* or the Supreme Personality of Godhead, because one cannot take his possessions with him. They remain here, and they will be lost. Either we leave the money or the money leaves us, but we will be separated. The best use of money as long as it is within our possession is to spend it to acquire and propagate Kṛṣṇa consciousness.

TEXT 32: "Thus, by the arrangement of the Supreme Personality of Godhead, the maintainer of kinsmen is put into a hellish condition to suffer for his sinful activities, like a man who has lost his wealth."

PURPORT: The example set herein is that the sinful person suffers just like a man who has lost his wealth. The human form of body is achieved by the conditioned soul after many, many births and is a very valuable asset. Instead of utilizing this life to get liberation, if one uses it simply for the purpose of maintaining his so-called family and therefore performs foolish and unauthorized action, he is compared to a man who has lost his wealth and who, upon losing it, laments. When wealth is lost, there is no use lamenting, but as long as there is wealth, one has to utilize it properly and thereby gain eternal profit. It may be argued that when a man leaves his money earned by sinful activities, he also leaves his sinful activities here with his money. But it is especially mentioned herein that by superior arrangement, although the man leaves behind his sinfully earned money, he carries the effect of it.

When a man steals some money, if he is caught and agrees to return it, he is not freed from the criminal punishment. By the law of the state, even though he returns the money, he has to undergo the punishment. Similarly, the money earned by a criminal process may be left by the man when dying, but by superior arrangement he carries with him the effect, and therefore he has to suffer hellish life.

TEXT 33: "Therefore a person who is very eager to maintain his family and kinsmen simply by black methods certainly goes to the darkest region of hell, which is known as Andha-tāmisra."

PURPORT: Three words in this verse are very significant. *Kevalena* means "only by black methods," *adharmeṇa* means "unrighteous" or "irreligious," and *kuṭumba-bharaṇa* means "family maintenance." Maintaining one's family is certainly the duty of a householder, but one should be eager to earn his livelihood by the prescribed method, as stated in the scriptures. In the *Bhagavad-gītā* it is described that the Lord has divided the social system into four classifications of castes, or *varṇas,* according to quality and work. Apart from the *Bhagavad-gītā,* in every society a man is known according to his quality and work. For example, when a man earns his livelihood constructing wooden furniture, he is called a carpenter, and a man who works with an anvil and iron is called a blacksmith. Similarly, a man who is engaged in the medical or engineering fields has a particular duty and designation. All these human activities have been divided by the Supreme Lord into four *varṇas,* namely the *brāhmaṇas* (intellectuals and priests), the *kṣatriyas* (warriors and administrators), the *vaiśyas* (merchants and farmers), and *śūdras* (manual laborers). In the *Bhagavad-gītā* and other Vedic scriptures, the specific duties of the *brāhmaṇas, kṣatriyas, vaiśyas,* and *śūdras* are mentioned.

One should work honestly according to his qualification. He should not earn his livelihood unfairly or in a way for which he is not qualified. If someone claims to be a *brāhmaṇa* and works as a priest, attracting people who expect to be enlightened about the spiritual way of life, but he is not qualified as a priest, then he is cheating the public. One should not earn one's livelihood by such unfair means. The same is applicable to a *kṣatriya* and a *vaiśya.* It is especially mentioned that the means of livelihood of those who are trying to advance in Kṛṣṇa consciousness must be very fair and uncomplicated. Here it is mentioned that he who earns his livelihood by unfair means (*kevalena*) is sent to the darkest hellish region. Otherwise, if one maintains his family by prescribed methods and honest means, there is no objection to one's being a family man.

TEXT 34: "Having gone through all the miserable, hellish conditions and having passed in a regular order through the lowest forms of animal life prior to human birth, and having thus been purged of one's sins, one is reborn again as a human being on this earth."

PURPORT: Just as a prisoner who has undergone troublesome prison life is set free again, the person who has always engaged in impious and mischievous activities is put into hellish conditions, and when he has undergone different hellish lives, namely those of lower animals like cats, dogs, and hogs, by the gradual process of evolution he again comes back as a human being. In the *Bhagavad-gītā* it is stated that even though a person engaged in the practice of the *yoga* system may not finish perfectly and may fall down for some reason or other, his next life as a human being is guaranteed. It is stated that such a person, who has fallen from the path of *yoga* practice, is given a chance in his next life to take birth in a very rich family or in a very pious family. It is interpreted that "rich family" refers to a big mercantile family because generally people who engage in business are very rich. One who engaged in the process of self-realization, or connecting with the Supreme Absolute Truth, but fell short is allowed to take birth in such a rich family, or he is allowed to take birth in the family of pious *brāhmaṇas;* either way, he is guaranteed to appear in human society in his next life.

It can be concluded that if someone is not willing to enter into hellish life, as in Tāmisra or Andha-tāmisra, then he must take to the process of Kṛṣṇa consciousness, which is the first-class *yoga* system, because even if one is unable to attain complete Kṛṣṇa consciousness in this life, he is guaranteed at least to take his next birth in a human family. He cannot be sent into a hellish condition. Kṛṣṇa consciousness is the purest life, and it protects all human beings from gliding down to hell to take birth in a family of dogs or hogs.

CHAPTER 3

THE PEACE FORMULA

The laws of nature work collectively, as well as individually. In the following brief but cogent statement, Śrīla Prabhupāda explains that if we want to break out of the tangled web of collective karma that is wreaking havoc in present-day society—if we want peace both collectively and individually—we need to take to Kṛṣṇa consciousness seriously.

The great mistake of modern civilization is to encroach upon others' property as though it were one's own and thereby create an unnecessary disturbance of the laws of nature. These laws are very strong. No living entity can violate them. Only one who is Kṛṣṇa conscious can easily overcome the stringent laws of nature and thus become happy and peaceful in the world.

As a state is protected by the department of law and order, so the state of the universe, of which this earth is only an insignificant fragment, is protected by the laws of nature. This material nature is one of the different potencies of God, who is the ultimate proprietor of everything that be. This earth is, therefore, the property of God, but we, the living entities, especially the so-called civilized human beings, are claiming God's property as our own under both an individual and collective false conception. If you want peace, you have to remove this false conception from your mind and from the world. This false claim of proprietorship by the human race on earth is partly or wholly the cause of all disturbances of peace on earth.

Foolish so-called civilized men are claiming proprietary rights on the property of God because they have now become godless. You cannot be happy and peaceful in a godless society. In the *Bhagavad-gītā* Lord Kṛṣṇa says that He is the factual enjoyer of all activities of the living entities, that He is the Supreme Lord of all universes, and that He is the well-wishing friend of all beings. When the people of the world know this as the formula for peace, it is then and there that peace will prevail.

Therefore, if you want peace at all, you will have to change your consciousness into Kṛṣṇa consciousness, both individually and collectively, by the simple process of chanting the holy name of God. This is the standard and recognized process for achieving peace in the world. We therefore recommend that everyone become Kṛṣṇa conscious by chanting Hare Kṛṣṇa, Hare Kṛṣṇa, Kṛṣṇa Kṛṣṇa, Hare Hare/ Hare Rāma, Hare Rāma, Rāma Rāma, Hare Hare.

This is practical, simple, and sublime. Five hundred years ago this formula was introduced in India by Lord Śrī Caitanya, and now it is available throughout the world. Take to this simple process of chanting as above mentioned, realize your factual position by reading the *Bhagavad-gītā As It Is,* and reestablish your lost relationship with Kṛṣṇa, God. Peace and prosperity will be the immediate worldwide result.

APPENDIXES

THE AUTHOR

His Divine Grace A. C. Bhaktivedanta Swami Prabhupāda appeared in this world in 1896 in Calcutta, India. He first met his spiritual master, Śrīla Bhaktisiddhānta Sarasvatī Gosvāmī, in Calcutta in 1922. Bhaktisiddhānta Sarasvatī, a prominent religious scholar and the founder of sixty-four Gauḍīya Maṭhas (Vedic institutes) in India, liked this educated young man and convinced him to dedicate his life to teaching Vedic knowledge. Śrīla Prabhupāda became his student and, in 1933, his formally initiated disciple.

At their first meeting Śrīla Bhaktisiddhānta Sarasvatī requested Śrīla Prabhupāda to broadcast Vedic knowledge in English. In the years that followed, Śrīla Prabhupāda wrote a commentary on the *Bhagavad-gītā,* assisted the Gauḍīya Maṭha in its work, and, in 1944, started *Back to Godhead,* an English fortnightly magazine. Single-handedly, Śrīla Prabhupāda edited it, typed the manuscripts, checked the galley proofs, and even distributed the individual copies. The magazine is now being continued by his disciples in the West.

In 1950 Śrīla Prabhupāda retired from married life, adopting the *vānaprastha* (retired) order to devote more time to his studies and writing. He traveled to the holy city of Vṛndāvana, where he lived in humble circumstances in the historic temple of Rādhā-Dāmodara. There he engaged for several years in deep study and writing. He accepted the renounced order of life (*sannyāsa*) in 1959. At Rādhā-Dāmodara, Śrīla Prabhupāda began work on his life's masterpiece: a multivolume commentated translation of the eighteen-thousand-verse *Śrīmad-Bhagavatam* (*Bhāgavata Purāṇa*). He also wrote *Easy Journey to Other Planets.*

After publishing three volumes of the *Bhāgavatam,* Śrīla Prabhupāda came to the United States, in September 1965, to fulfill the mission of his spiritual master. Subsequently, His Divine Grace wrote more than fifty volumes of authoritative commentated translations and summary studies of the philosophical and religious classics of India.

When he first arrived by freighter in New York City, Śrīla Prabhupāda was practically penniless. Only after almost a year of great difficulty did he establish the International Society for Krishna Consciousness, in July of 1966. Before he passed away on November 14, 1977, he had guided the Society and seen it grow to a worldwide confederation of more than one hundred *āśramas,* schools, temples, institutes, and farm communities.

In 1972 His Divine Grace introduced the Vedic system of primary and secondary education in the West by founding the *gurukula* school in Dallas, Texas. Since then his disciples have established similar schools throughout the United States and the rest of the world.

Śrīla Prabhupāda also inspired the construction of several large international cultural centers in India. The center at Śrīdhāma Māyāpur is the site for a planned spiritual city, an ambitions project for which construction will extend over many years to come. In Vṛndāvana are the magnificent Kṛṣṇa-Balarāma Temple and International Guesthouse, *gurukula* school, and Śrīla

Prabhupāda Memorial and Museum. There is also a major cultural and educational center in Bombay. Major centers are planned in Delhi and in a dozen other important locations on the Indian subcontinent.

Śrīla Prabhupāda's most significant contribution, however, is his books. Highly respected by scholars for their authority, depth, and clarity, they are used as textbooks in numerous college courses. His writings have been translated into over fifty languages. The Bhaktivedanta Book Trust, established in 1972 to publish the works of His Divine Grace, has thus become the world's largest publisher of books in the field of Indian religion and philosophy.

In just twelve years, despite his advanced age, Śrīla Prabhupāda circled the globe fourteen times on lecture tours that took him to six continents. Yet this vigorous schedule did not slow his prolific literary output. His writings constitute a veritable library of Vedic philosophy, religion, literature, and culture.

KṚṢṆA CONSCIOUSNESS AT HOME

From what we've read in *The Laws of Nature,* it's clear how important it is for everyone to practice Kṛṣṇa consciousness, devotional service to Lord Kṛṣṇa. Of course, living in the association of Kṛṣṇa's devotees in a temple or *āśrama* makes it easier to practice devotional service. But if you're determined, you can follow at home the teachings of Kṛṣṇa consciousness and thus convert your home into a temple.

Spiritual life, like material life, means practical activity. The difference is that whereas we perform material activities for the benefit of ourselves or those we consider ours, we perform spiritual activities for the benefit of Lord Kṛṣṇa, under the guidance of the scriptures and the spiritual master. The key is to accept the guidance of the scripture and the *guru.* Kṛṣṇa declares in the *Bhagavad-gītā* that a person can achieve neither happiness nor the supreme destination of life—going back to Godhead, back to Lord Kṛṣṇa—if he or she does not follow the injunctions of the scriptures. And *how* to follow the scriptural rules by engaging in practical service to the Lord—that is explained by a bona fide spiritual master. Without following the instructions of a spiritual master who is in an authorized chain of disciplic succession coming from Kṛṣṇa Himself, we cannot make spiritual progress. The practices outlined here are the timeless practices of *bhakti-yoga* as given by the foremost spiritual master and exponent of Kṛṣṇa consciousness in our time, His Divine

Grace A. C. Bhaktivedanta Swami Prabhupāda, founder-*ācārya* of theInternational Society for Krishna Consciousness (ISKCON).

The purpose of spiritual knowledge is to bring us closer to God, or Kṛṣṇa. Kṛṣṇa says in the *Bhagavad-gītā* (18.55), *bhaktyā māṁ abhijānāti:* "I can be known only by devotional service." Knowledge guides us in proper action. Spiritual knowledge directs us to satisfy the desires of Kṛṣṇa through practical engagements in His loving service. Without practical application, theoretical knowledge is of little value.

Spiritual knowledge is meant to direct us in all aspects of life. We should endeavor, therefore, to organize our lives in such a way as to follow Kṛṣṇa's teachings as far as possible. We should try to do our best, to do more than is simply convenient. Then it will be possible for us to rise to the transcendental plane of Kṛṣṇa consciousness, even while living far from a temple.

Chanting Hare Kṛṣṇa

The first principle in devotional service is to chant the Hare Kṛṣṇa *mahā-mantra* (*mahā* means "great"; *mantra* means "sound that liberates the mind from ignorance"):

Hare Kṛṣṇa, Hare Kṛṣṇa, Kṛṣṇa Kṛṣṇa, Hare Hare
Hare Rāma, Hare Rāma, Rāma Rāma, Hare Hare

You can chant these holy names of the Lord anywhere and at any time, but it is best to set a specific time of the day to regularly chant. Early morning hours are ideal.

The chanting can be done in two ways: singing the *mantra*, called *kīrtana* (usually done in a group), and saying the *mantra* to oneself, called *japa* (which literally means "to speak softly"). Concentrate on hearing the sound of the holy names. As you chant, pronounce the names clearly and distinctly, addressing Kṛṣṇa in a prayerful mood. When your mind wanders, bring it back to the sound of the Lord's names. Chanting is a prayer to Kṛṣṇa that means "O energy of the Lord [Hare], O all-attractive Lord [Kṛṣṇa], O Supreme Enjoyer [Rāma], please engage me in Your service." The more attentively and sincerely you chant these names of God, the more spiritual progress you will make.

Since God is all-powerful and all-merciful, He has kindly made it very easy for us to chant His names, and He has also invested all His powers in them. Therefore the names of God and God Himself are identical. This means that when we chant the holy names of Kṛṣṇa and Rāma we are directly associating with God and being purified. Therefore we should always try to chant with devotion and reverence. The Vedic literature states that Lord Kṛṣṇa is personally dancing on your tongue when you chant His holy name.

When you chant alone, it is best to chant on *japa* beads (available from the Bhaktivedanta Book Trust, at one of the addresses given in the advertisement at the end of this book). This not only helps you fix your attention on the holy name, but it also helps you count the number of times you chant the *mantra* daily. Each strand of *japa* beads contains 108 small beads and one large bead, the head bead. Begin on a bead next to the head bead and gently roll it between the thumb and middle finger of your right hand as you chant the full Hare Kṛṣṇa *mantra.* Then move to the next bead and repeat the process. In this way, chant on each of the 108 beads until you reach the head bead again. This is one round of *japa*. Then, without chanting on the head bead, reverse the beads and start your second round on the last bead you chanted on.

Initiated devotees vow before the spiritual master to chant at least sixteen rounds of the Hare Kṛṣṇa *mantra* daily. But even if you can chant only one round a day, the principle is that once you commit yourself to chanting that round, you should try to complete it every day without fail. When

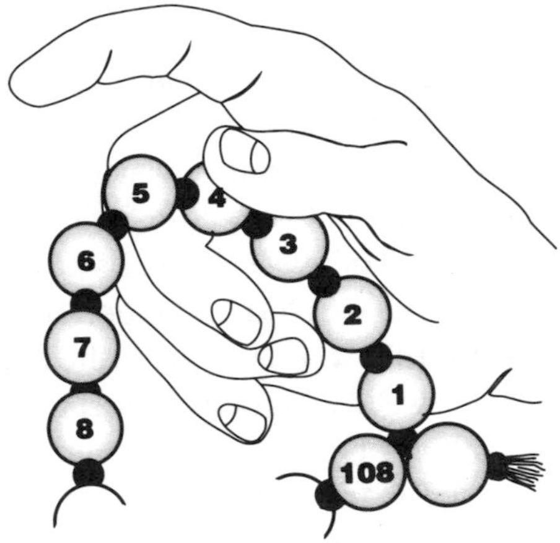

you feel you can chant more, then increase the minimum number of rounds you chant each day—but don't fall below that number. You can chant more than your fixed number, but you should maintain a set minimum each day. (Please note that the beads are sacred and therefore should never touch the ground or be put in an unclean place. To keep your beads clean, it's best to carry them in a special bead bag, also available from the Bhaktivedanta Book Trust.)

Aside from chanting *japa,* you can also sing the Lord's holy names in *kīrtana*. While you can perform *kīrtana* individually, it is generally performed with others. A melodious *kīrtana* with family or friends is sure to enliven everyone. ISKCON devotees use traditional melodies and instruments, especially in the temple, but you can chant to any melody and use any musical instruments to accompany your chanting. As Lord Caitanya said, "There are no hard and fast rules for chanting Hare Kṛṣṇa." One thing you might want to do, however, is order some *kīrtana* and *japa* audiotapes from the Bhaktivedanta Book Trust.

Setting Up Your Altar

You'll likely find that *japa* and *kīrtana* are more effective when done before an altar. Lord Kṛṣṇa and His pure devotees are so kind that they allow us to worship them even through their pictures. It's something like mailing a letter: You can't mail a letter by

placing it in just any box; you must use the mailbox authorized by the government. Similarly, we cannot imagine a picture of God and worship that, but we can worship the authorized picture of God, and Kṛṣṇa accepts our worship through that picture.

Setting up an altar at home means receiving the Lord and His pure devotees as your most honored guests. Where should you set up the altar? Well, how would you seat a guest? An ideal place would be clean, well lit, and free from drafts and household disturbances. Your guest, of course, would need a comfortable chair, but for the picture of Kṛṣṇa's form a wall shelf, a mantelpiece, a corner table, or the top shelf of a bookcase will do. You wouldn't seat a guest in your home and then ignore him; you'd provide a place for yourself to sit, too, where you could comfortably face him and enjoy his company. So don't make your altar inaccessible.

What do you need to set up your altar? Here are the essentials:

1. A picture of Śrīla Prabhupāda.
2. A picture of Lord Caitanya and His associates.
3. A picture of Śrī Śrī Rādhā-Kṛṣṇa.

In addition, you may want an altar cloth, water cups (one for each picture), candles with holders, a special plate for offering food, a small bell, incense, an incense holder, and fresh flowers, which you may offer in vases or simply place before each picture. If you're interested in more elaborate Deity worship, ask any of the ISKCON devotees or write to the Bhaktivedanta Book Trust.

The first person we worship on the altar is the spiritual master. The spiritual master is not God. Only God is God. But because the spiritual master is His dearmost servant, God has empowered him, and therefore he deserves the same respect as that given to God. He links the disciple with God and teaches him the process of *bhakti-yoga.* He is God's ambassador to the material world. When a president sends an ambassador to a foreign country, the ambassador receives the same respect as that accorded the president, and the ambassador's words are as authoritative as the president's. Similarly, we should respect the spiritual master as we would God, and revere his words as we would His.

There are two main kinds of *gurus:* the instructing *guru* and the initiating *guru.* Everyone who takes up the process of *bhakti-yoga* as a result of coming in contact with ISKCON owes an immense debt of gratitude to Śrīla Prabhupāda. Before Śrīla Prabhupāda left India in 1965 to spread Kṛṣṇa consciousness abroad, almost no one outside India knew anything about the practice of pure devotional service to Lord Kṛṣṇa. Therefore, everyone who has learned of the process through his books, his *Back to Godhead* magazine, his tapes, or contact with his followers should offer respect to Śrīla Prabhupāda. As the founder and spiritual guide of the International Society for Krishna Consciousness, he is the instructing *guru* of us all.

As you progress in *bhakti-yoga,* you may eventually want to accept initiation. Before he left this world in 1977, Śrīla Prabhupāda authorized a system in which advanced and qualified devotees would carry on his work by initiating disciples in accordance with his instructions. At present there are many spiritual masters in ISKCON. To learn how you can get in touch with them for spiritual guidance, ask a devotee at your nearby temple, or write to the president of one of the ISKCON centers listed at the end of this book.

The second picture on your altar should be one of the *pañca-tattva,* Lord Caitanya and His four leading associates. Lord Caitanya is the incarnation of God for this age. He is Kṛṣṇa Himself, descended in the form of His own devotee to teach us how to surrender to Him, specifically by chanting His holy names and performing other activities of *bhakti-yoga.* Lord Caitanya is the most merciful incarnation, for He makes it easy for anyone to attain love of God through the chanting of the Hare Kṛṣṇa *mantra*.

And of course your altar should have a picture of the Supreme Personality of Godhead, Lord Śrī Kṛṣṇa, with His eternal consort, Śrīmatī Rādhārāṇī. Śrīmatī Rādhārāṇī is Kṛṣṇa's spiritual potency. She is devotional service personified, and devotees always take shelter of Her to learn how to serve Kṛṣṇa.

You can arrange the pictures in a triangle, with the picture of Śrīla Prabhupāda on the left, the picture of Lord Caitanya and His associates on the right, and the picture of Rādhā and Kṛṣṇa, which, if possible, should be slightly larger than the others, on a small raised platform behind and in the center. Or you can hang the picture of Rādhā and Kṛṣṇa on the wall above.

Carefully clean the altar each morning. Cleanliness is essential in Deity worship. Remember, you wouldn't neglect to clean the room of an important guest, and when you establish an altar you invite Kṛṣṇa and His pure devotees to reside as the most exalted guests in your home. If you have water cups, rinse them out and fill them with fresh water daily. Then place them conveniently close to the pictures. You should remove flowers in vases as soon as they're slightly wilted, or daily if you've offered them at the base of the pictures. You should offer fresh incense at least once a day, and, if possible, light candles and place them near the pictures when you're chanting before the altar.

Please try the things we've suggested so far. It's very simple, really: If you try to love God, you'll gradually realize how much He loves you. That's the essence of *bhakti-yoga.*

Prasādam: How to Eat Spiritually

By His immense transcendental energies, Kṛṣṇa can actually convert matter into spirit. If we place an iron rod in a fire, before long the rod becomes red hot and acts just like fire. In the same way, food prepared for and offered to Kṛṣṇa with love and devotion becomes completely spiritualized. Such food is called Kṛṣṇa *prasādam,* which means "the mercy of Lord Kṛṣṇa."

Eating *prasādam* is a fundamental practice of *bhakti-yoga.* In other forms of *yoga* one must artificially repress the senses, but the *bhakti-yogī* can engage his or her senses in a variety of pleasing spiritual activities, such as tasting delicious food offered to Lord Kṛṣṇa. In this way the senses gradually become spiritualized and bring the devotee more and more transcendental pleasure by being engaged in devotional service. Such spiritual pleasure far surpasses any kind of material experience.

Lord Caitanya said of *prasādam,* "Everyone has tasted these foods before. However, now that they have been prepared for Kṛṣṇa and offered to Him with devotion, these foods have acquired extraordinary tastes and uncommon fragrances. Just taste them and see the difference in the experience! Apart from the taste, even the fragrance pleases the mind and makes one forget any other fragrance. Therefore, it should be understood that the spiritual nectar of Kṛṣṇa's lips must have touched these ordinary foods and imparted to them all their transcendental qualities."

Eating only food offered to Kṛṣṇa is the perfection of vegetarianism. In itself, being a vegetarian is not enough; after all, even pigeons and monkeys are vegetarians. But when we go beyond vegetarianism to a diet of *prasādam,* our eating becomes helpful in achieving the goal of human life—reawakening the soul's original relationship with God. In the *Bhagavad-gītā* Lord Kṛṣṇa says that unless one eats only food that has been offered to Him in sacrifice, one will suffer the reactions of *karma.*

How to Prepare and Offer Prasādam

As you walk down the supermarket aisles selecting the foods you will offer to Kṛṣṇa, you need to know what is offerable and what is not. In the *Bhagavad-gītā,* Lord Kṛṣṇa states, "If one offers Me with love and devotion a leaf, a flower, a fruit, or water, I will accept it." From this verse it is understood that we can offer Kṛṣṇa foods prepared from milk products, vegetables, fruits, nuts, and grains. (Write to the Bhaktivedanta Book Trust for one of the many Hare Kṛṣṇa cookbooks.) Meat, fish, and eggs are not offerable. And a few vegetarian items are also forbidden—garlic and onions, for example, which are in the mode of darkness. (*Hing,* or asafetida, is a tasty substitute for them in cooking and is available at most Indian groceries or from the Bhaktivedanta Book Trust.) Nor can you offer to Kṛṣṇa coffee or tea that contain caffeine. If you like these beverages, purchase caffeine-free coffee and herbal teas.

While shopping, be aware that you may find meat, fish, and egg products mixed with other foods; so be sure to read labels carefully. For instance, some brands of yogurt and sour cream contain gelatin, a substance made from the horns, hooves, and bones of slaughtered animals. Also, make sure the cheese you buy contains no rennet, an enzyme extracted from the stomach tissues of slaughtered calves. Most hard cheese sold in America contains rennet, so be careful about any cheese you can't verify as rennetless.

Also avoid foods cooked by nondevotees. According to the subtle laws of nature, the cook acts upon the food not only physically but mentally as well. Food thus becomes an agent for subtle influences on your consciousness. The principle is the same as that at work with a painting: a painting is not simply a collection of strokes on a canvas but an expression of the artist's state of mind, which affects the viewer. So if you eat food cooked by nondevotees—employees working in a factory, for example—then you're sure to absorb a dose of materialism and *karma*. So as far as possible use only fresh, natural ingredients.

In preparing food, cleanliness is the most important principle. Nothing impure should be offered to God; so keep your kitchen very clean. Always wash your hands thoroughly before entering the kitchen. While preparing food, do not taste it, for you are cooking the meal not for yourself but for the pleasure of Kṛṣṇa. Arrange portions of the food on dinnerware kept especially for this purpose; no one but the Lord should eat from these dishes. The easiest way to offer food is simply to pray, "My dear Lord Kṛṣṇa, please accept this food," and to chant each of the following prayers three times while ringing a bell (see the Sanskrit Pronunciation Guide on page 104):

1. Prayer to Śrīla Prabhupāda:

nama oṁ viṣṇu-pādāya kṛṣṇa-preṣṭhāya bhū-tale
śrīmate bhaktivedānta-svāmin iti nāmine

namas te sārasvate deve gaura-vāṇī-pracāriṇe
nirviśeṣa-śūnyavādi-pāścātya-deśa-tāriṇe

"I offer my respectful obeisances unto His Divine Grace A. C. Bhaktivedanta Swami Prabhupāda, who is very dear to Lord Kṛṣṇa, having taken shelter at His lotus feet. Our respectful obeisances are unto you, O spiritual master, servant of Bhaktisiddhānta Sarasvatī Gosvāmī. You are kindly preaching the message of

Lord Caitanyadeva and delivering the Western countries, which are filled with impersonalism and voidism."

2. Prayer to Lord Caitanya:

namo mahā-vadānyāya kṛṣṇa-prema-pradāya te
kṛṣṇāya kṛṣṇa-caitanya-nāmne gaura-tviṣe namaḥ

"O most munificent incarnation! You are Kṛṣṇa Himself appearing as Śrī Kṛṣṇa Caitanya Mahāprabhu. You have assumed the golden color of Śrīmatī Rādhārāṇī, and You are widely distributing pure love of Kṛṣṇa. We offer our respectful obeisances unto You."

3. Prayer to Lord Kṛṣṇa:

namo brahmaṇya-devāya go-brāhmaṇa-hitāya ca
jagad-dhitāya kṛṣṇāya govindāya namo namaḥ

"I offer my respectful obeisances unto Lord Kṛṣṇa, who is the worshipable Deity for all *brāhmaṇas*, the well-wisher of the cows and the *brāhmaṇas*, and the benefactor of the whole world. I offer my repeated obeisances to the Personality of Godhead, known as Kṛṣṇa and Govinda."

Remember that the real purpose of preparing and offering food to the Lord is to show your devotion and gratitude to Him. Kṛṣṇa accepts your devotion, not the physical offering itself. God is complete in Himself—He doesn't need anything—but out of His immense kindness He allows us to offer food to Him so that we can develop our love for Him.

After offering the food to the Lord, wait at least five minutes for Him to partake of the preparations. Then you should transfer the food from the special dinnerware and wash the dishes and utensils you used for the offering. Now you and any guests may eat the *prasādam.* While you eat, try to appreciate the spiritual value of the food. Remember that because Kṛṣṇa has accepted it, it is nondifferent from Him, and therefore by eating it you will become purified.

Everything you offer on your altar becomes *prasādam,* the mercy of the Lord. The flowers, the incense, the water, the food—everything you offer for the Lord's pleasure becomes spiritualized. The Lord enters into the offerings, and thus the remnants are nondifferent from Him. So you should not only deeply respect the things you've offered, but you should distribute them to others as well. Distribution of *prasādam* is an essential part of Deity worship.

Everyday Life: The Four Regulative Principles

Anyone serious about progressing in Kṛṣṇa consciousness must try to avoid the following four sinful activities:

1. **Eating meat, fish, or eggs.** These foods are saturated with the modes of passion and ignorance and therefore cannot be offered to the Lord. A person who eats these foods participates in a conspiracy of violence against helpless animals and thus stops his spiritual progress dead in its tracks.

2. **Gambling.** Gambling invariably puts one into anxiety and fuels greed, envy, and anger.

3. **The use of intoxicants.** Drugs, alcohol, and to-

bacco, as well as any drinks or foods containing caffeine, cloud the mind, overstimulate the senses, and make it impossible to understand or follow the principles of *bhakti-yoga*.

4. **Illicit sex.** This is sex outside of marriage or sex in marriage for any purpose other than procreation. Sex for pleasure compels one to identify with the body and takes one far from Kṛṣṇa consciousness. The scriptures teach that sex is the most powerful force binding us to the material world. Anyone serious about advancing in Kṛṣṇa consciousness should minimize sex or eliminate it entirely.

Engagement in Practical Devotional Service

Everyone must do some kind of work, but if you work only for yourself you must accept the karmic reactions of that work. As Lord Kṛṣṇa says in the *Bhagavad-gītā* (3.9), "Work done as a sacrifice for Viṣṇu [Kṛṣṇa] has to be performed. Otherwise work binds one to the material world."

You needn't change your occupation, except if you're now engaged in a sinful job such as working as a butcher or bartender. If you're a writer, write for Kṛṣṇa; if you're an artist, create for Kṛṣṇa; if you're a secretary, type for Kṛṣṇa. You may also directly help the temple in your spare time, and you should sacrifice some of the fruits of your work by contributing a portion of your earnings to help maintain the temple and propagate Kṛṣṇa consciousness. Some devotees living outside the temple buy Hare Kṛṣṇa literature and distribute it to their friends and associates, or they engage in a variety of services at the temple. There is also a wide network of devotees who gather in each other's homes for chanting, worship, and study. Write to your local temple or the Society's secretary to learn of any such programs near you.

Additional Devotional Principles

There are many more devotional practices that can help you become Kṛṣṇa conscious. Here are two vital ones:

Studying Hare Kṛṣṇa literature. Śrīla Prabhupāda, the founder-*ācārya* of ISKCON, dedicated much of his time to writing books such as the *Śrīmad-Bhāgavatam,* the source of the chapter describing the fate of the sinful family man. Hearing the words—or reading the writings—of a realized spiritual master is an essential spiritual practice. So try to set aside some time every day to read Śrīla Prabhupāda's books. You can get a free catalog of available books and tapes from the Bhaktivedanta Book Trust.

Associating with devotees. Śrīla Prabhupāda established the Hare Kṛṣṇa movement to give people in general the chance to associate with devotees of the Lord. This is the best way to gain faith in the process of Kṛṣṇa consciousness and become enthusiastic in devotional service. Conversely, maintaining intimate connections with nondevotees slows one's spiritual progress. So try to visit the Hare Kṛṣṇa center nearest you as often as possible.

In Closing

The beauty of Kṛṣṇa consciousness is that you can take as much as you're ready for. Kṛṣṇa Himself promises in the *Bhagavad-gītā* (2.40), "There is no loss or diminution in this endeavor, and even a little advancement on this path protects one from the most fearful type of danger." So bring Kṛṣṇa into your daily life, and we guarantee you'll feel the benefit.

Hare Kṛṣṇa!

SANSKRIT PRONUNCIATION GUIDE

The system of transliteration used in this book conforms to a system that scholars have accepted to indicate the pronunciation of each sound in the Sanskrit language.

The short vowel **a** is pronounced like the **u** in b**u**t, long **ā** like the **a** in f**a**r. Short **i** is pronounced as in p**i**n, long **ī** as in p**i**que, short **u** as in p**u**ll, and long **ū** as in r**u**le. The vowel **ṛ** is pronounced like the **ri** in **ri**m, **e** like the **ey** in th**ey**, **o** like the **o** in g**o, ai** like the **ai** in **ai**sle, and **au** like the **ow** in h**ow**. The *anusvāra* (**ṁ**) is pronounced like the **n** in the French word *bo***n**, and *visarga* (**ḥ**) is pronounced as a final **h** sound. At the end of a couplet, **aḥ** is pronounced **aha**, and **iḥ** is pronounced **ihi**.

The guttural consonants—**k, kh, g, gh,** and **ṅ**—are pronounced from the throat in much the same manner as in English. **K** is pronounced as in **k**ite, **kh** as in Ec**kh**art, **g** as in **g**ive, **gh** as in di**g h**ard, and **ṅ** as in si**ng.**

The palatal consonants—**c, ch, j, jh,** and **ñ**—are pronounced with the tongue touching the firm ridge behind the teeth. **C** is pronounced as in **ch**air, **ch** as in staun**ch-h**eart, **j** as in **j**oy, **jh** as in he**dgeh**og, and **ñ** as in ca**n**yon.

The cerebral consonants—**ṭ, ṭh, ḍ, ḍh,** and **ṇ**—are pronounced with the tip of the tongue turned up and drawn back against the dome of the palate. **Ṭ** is pronounced as in **t**ub, **ṭh** as in ligh**t-h**eart, **ḍ** as in **d**ove, **ḍh** as in re**d-h**ot, and **ṇ** as in **n**ut. The dental consonants—**t, th, d, dh,** and **n**—are pronounced in the same manner as the cerebrals, but with the forepart of the tongue against the teeth.

The labial consonants—**p, ph, b, bh,** and **m**—are pronounced with the lips. **P** is pronounced as in **p**ine, **ph** as in u**ph**ill, **b** as in **b**ird, **bh** as in ru**b-h**ard, and **m** as in **m**other.

The semivowels—**y, r, l,** and **v**—are pronounced as in **y**es, **r**un, **l**ight, and **v**ine respectively. The sibilants—**ś, ṣ,** and **s**—are pronounced, respectively, as in the German word **s***prechen* and the English words **sh**ine and **s**un. The letter **h** is pronounced as in **h**ome.

WHAT IS THE INTERNATIONAL SOCIETY FOR KRISHNA CONSCIOUSNESS?

The International Society for Krishna Consciousness (ISKCON), popularly known as the Hare Kṛṣṇa movement, is a worldwide association of devotees of Kṛṣṇa, the Supreme Personality of Godhead. God is known by many names according to His different qualities and activities. In the Bible He is known as Jehovah ("the almighty one"), in the Koran as Allah ("the great one"), and in the *Bhagavad-gītā* as Kṛṣṇa, a Sanskrit name meaning "the all-attractive one."

The movement's main purpose is to promote the well-being of human society by teaching the science of God consciousness (Kṛṣṇa consciousness) according to the timeless Vedic scriptures of India.

Many leading figures in the international religious and academic community have affirmed the movement's authenticity. Diana L. Eck, professor of comparative religion and Indian studies at Harvard University, describes the movement as a "tradition that commands a respected place in the religious life of humankind."

In 1965, His Divine Grace A. C. Bhaktivedanta Swami, known to his followers as Śrīla Prabhupāda, brought Kṛṣṇa consciousness to America. On the day he landed in America, he penned these words in his diary: "My dear Lord Kṛṣṇa, I am sure that when this transcendental message penetrates their hearts, they will certainly feel gladdened and thus become liberated from all unhappy conditions of life." He was sixty-nine years old, alone and with few resources, but the wealth of spiritual knowledge and devotion he possessed was an unwavering source of strength and inspiration.

"At a very advanced age, when most people would be resting on their laurels," writes Harvey Cox, Harvard University theologian and author, "Śrīla Prabhupāda harkened to the mandate of his own spiritual teacher and set out on the difficult and demanding voyage to America. Śrīla Prabhupāda is, of course, only one of thousands of teachers. But in another sense, he is one in a thousand, maybe one in a million."

In 1966, Śrīla Prabhupāda founded the International Society for Kṛṣṇa Consciousness, which became the formal name for the Hare Kṛṣṇa movement.

Astonishing Growth

In the years that followed, Śrīla Prabhupāda gradually attracted tens of thousands of followers, started more than a hundred temples and ashrams, and published scores of books. His achievement is remarkable in that he transplanted India's ancient spiritual culture to the twentieth-century Western world.

New devotees of Kṛṣṇa soon became highly visible in all the major cities around the world by their public chanting and their distribution of Śrīla Prabhupāda's books of Vedic knowledge. They began staging joyous cultural festivals throughout the year and serving millions of plates of delicious food offered to Kṛṣṇa (known as *prasādam*) throughout the world. As a result, ISKCON has significantly influenced the lives of hundreds of thousands of people. The late A. L. Basham, one of the world's leading authorities on Indian history and culture, wrote, "The Hare Kṛṣṇa movement arose out of next to nothing in less than twenty years and has become known all over the West. This is an important fact in the history of the Western world."

Five Thousand Years of Spiritual Wisdom

Scholars worldwide have acclaimed Śrīla Prabhupāda's translations of Vedic literature. Garry Gelade, a professor at Oxford University's Department of Philosophy, wrote of them: "These texts are to be treasured. No one of whatever faith or philosophical persuasion who reads these books with an open mind can fail to be moved and impressed." And Dr. Larry Shinn, Dean of the College of Arts and Sciences at Bucknell University, wrote, "Prabhupāda's personal piety gave him real authority. He exhibited complete command of the scriptures, an unusual depth of realization, and an outstanding personal example, because he actually lived what he taught."

The best known of the Vedic texts, the *Bhagavad-gītā* ("Song of God"), is the philosophical basis for the Hare Kṛṣṇa movement. Dating back 5,000 years, it is sacred to more than 700 million people today.

This exalted work has been praised by scholars and leaders the world over. Gandhi said, "When doubts haunt me, when disappointments stare me in the face and I see not one ray of hope, I turn to the *Bhagavad-gītā* and find a verse to comfort me." Ralph Waldo Emerson wrote, "It was the first of books; it was as if an empire spoke to us, nothing small or unworthy, but large, serene, consistent, the voice of an old intelligence which in another age and climate had pondered and thus disposed of the same questions which exercise us." It is not surprising to anyone familiar with the *Gītā* that Henry David Thoreau said, "In the morning I bathe my intellect in the stupendous and cosmogonal philosophy of the *Bhagavad-gītā*."

Lord Kṛṣṇa teaches in the *Bhagavad-gītā* that we are not these temporary material bodies but spirit souls, or conscious entities, and that we can find genuine peace and happiness only in spiritual devotion to God. The *Gītā* and other well-known world scriptures recommend that people joyfully chant God's holy names, such as Kṛṣṇa, Allah, and Jehovah.

A Sixteenth-Century Incarnation of Kṛṣṇa

Lord Śrī Caitanya Mahāprabhu, a sixteenth-century full incarnation of Kṛṣṇa, popularized the chanting of God's names all over India. He constantly sang these names of God, as prescribed in the Vedic literatures: Hare Kṛṣṇa, Hare Kṛṣṇa, Kṛṣṇa Kṛṣṇa, Hare Hare/ Hare Rāma, Hare Rāma, Rāma Rāma, Hare Hare. This Hare Kṛṣṇa chant, or *mantra,* is a transcendental sound vibration. It purifies the mind and awakens the dormant love of God that resides in the hearts of all living beings. Lord Caitanya requested His followers to spread the chanting to every town and village of the world.

Anyone can take part in the chanting of Hare Kṛṣṇa and learn the science of spiritual devotion by studying the *Bhagavad-gītā*. This easy and practical process of self-realization will awaken our natural state of peace and happiness.

Hare Kṛṣṇa Lifestyles

The devotees seen dancing and chanting in the streets, dressed in traditional Indian robes, are for the most part full-time students of the Hare Kṛṣṇa movement. The vast majority of followers, however, live and work in the general community, practicing Kṛṣṇa consciousness in their homes and attending temples on a regular basis.

Full-time devotees throughout the world number about 3,000, with 200,000 congregational members. The movement comprises 167 temples, 40 rural communities, 26 schools, and 45 restaurants in 71 countries.

In order to revive humanity's inherent natural spiritual principles of compassion, truthfulness, cleanliness, and austerity, and to master the mind and the material senses, devotees also follow these four regulations:

1. No eating of meat, fish, or eggs.
2. No gambling.
3. No illicit sex.
4. No intoxication of any kind, including tobacco, coffee, and tea.

According to the *Bhagavad-gītā,* indulgence in the above activities disrupts our physical, mental, and spiritual well-being and increases anxiety and conflict in society.

A Philosophy for Everyone

The philosophy of the Hare Kṛṣṇa movement (a monotheistic tradition) is summarized in the following eight points:

1. By sincerely cultivating an authentic spiritual science, we can become free from anxiety and achieve a state of pure, unending, blissful consciousness.

2. Each of us is not the material body but an eternal spirit soul, part and parcel of God (Kṛṣṇa). As such, we are all interrelated through Kṛṣṇa, our common father.

3. Kṛṣṇa is eternal, all-knowing, omnipresent, all-powerful, and all-attractive. He is the seed-giving father of all living beings and the sustaining energy of the universe. He is the source of all incarnations of God, including Lord Buddha and Lord Jesus Christ.

4. The *Vedas* are the oldest scriptures in the world. The essence of the *Vedas* is found in the *Bhagavad-gītā,* a literal record of Kṛṣṇa's words spoken 5,000 years ago in India. The goal of Vedic knowledge—and of all religions—is to achieve love of God.

5. We can perfectly understand the knowledge of self-realization through the instructions of a genuine spiritual master—one who is free from selfish motives and whose mind is firmly fixed in meditation on Kṛṣṇa.

6. All that we eat should first be offered to Kṛṣṇa with a prayer. In this way Kṛṣṇa accepts the offering and blesses it for our purification.

7. Rather than living in a self-centered way, we should act for the pleasure of Kṛṣṇa. This is known as *bhakti-yoga,* the science of devotional service.

8. The most effective means for achieving God consciousness in this age of Kali, or quarrel, is to chant the holy names of the Lord: Hare Kṛṣṇa, Hare Kṛṣṇa, Kṛṣṇa Kṛṣṇa, Hare Hare/ Hare Rāma, Hare Rāma, Rāma Rāma, Hare Hare.

INDEX

Abortion, 68
Absolute Truth
knowledge of, via spiritual master, 42
understood via devotional service 48
Ācārya defined, 16
Adharmeṇa defined, 75
Airplanes, Vedic, 45
Analogies
airplane & earth, 14
airplane & universe, 19
airplane with pilot & body with soul, 19
cloud & ignorant person, 51
cloud & material energy, 18–19
coat and pants & body, 33
criminal & sinner, 9
disease & ignorance, 7
dog & invalid, 63
elephant & Absolute Truth, 48–9
fire emanating heat and light & Supreme Lord emanating spiritual and material energies, 18
gold & God, 14–15
lamb & Kṛṣṇa, 8
lion & death, 8
lion & Kṛṣṇa, 8
Los Angeles & body, 11–12
mathematics & *Vedas,* 24
million dollars & human body, 37–38
moon & Kṛṣṇa, 23
motorcar & body, 33
old ox & old family man, 62
prison & family life, 58
prison house & material world, 22
prisoner & sinner, 76
rope & modes of nature, 2
serpents & senses, 48

Analogies (*continued*)
shackles & woman and children, 58
sparks and fire & living entities and Lord, 27
state & universe, 79
sun & Absolute Truth, 48
sun & Kṛṣṇa, 18, 23
wind & time, 51
Andha-tāmisra hell, 70–71, 75, 77
Antaraṅgā śakti defined, 28
Apareyam itas tv anyāṁ quoted 19
Asat defined, 57
Ātma-tattva defined, 6
Āvaraṇātmikā defined, 54–5
Avidyā
absorption in, result of, 44
defined 1

Badarikāśrama, 44
Bahiraṅgā śakti defined, 28
Bahunāṁ janmanām ante quoted, 45
Bandha defined, 3
Bhagavad-gītā cited
on fate of unsuccessful *yogī,* 77
on Kṛṣṇa as supreme enjoyer, proprietor, & friend, 80
on living entities as Lord's superior energy, 11
on madness via lust, 68
on material energy as insurmountable, 2
on material world as place of misery, 59
on *prasādam,* value of, 7
on thoughts at death, 65
on *varṇāśrama,* 75
on Vivasvān as sun-god, 46

ISKCON Centers Around the World

June 1991

NORTH AMERICA

CANADA

Montreal, Quebec—1626 Pie IX Boulevard, H1V 2C5/ Tel. (514) 521-1301
Ottawa, Ontario—212 Somerset St. E., K1N 6V4/ Tel. (613) 233-1884
Regina, Saskatchewan—1279 Retallack St., S4T 2H8/ Tel. (306) 525-1640
Toronto, Ontario—243 Avenue Rd., M5R 2J6/ Tel. (416) 922-5415
Vancouver, B.C.—5462 S.E. Marine Dr., Burnaby V5J 3G8/ Tel. (604) 433-9728

FARM COMMUNITY

Ashcroft, B.C.—Saranagati Dhama, Box 99, Ashcroft, B.C. V0K 1A0

RESTAURANTS

Toronto—Hare Krishna Dining Room (at ISKCON Toronto)
Vancouver—Hare Krishna Buffet (at ISKCON Vancouver)

U.S.A.

Atlanta, Georgia—1287 Ponce de Leon Ave. N.E., 30306/ Tel. (404) 377- 8680
Baltimore, Maryland—200 Bloomsbury Ave., Catonsville, 21228/ Tel. (301) 744-9537
Boise, Idaho—1615 Martha St., 83706/ Tel. (208) 344-4274
Boulder, Colorado—917 Pleasant St., 80302/ Tel. (303) 444-7005
Boston, Massachusetts—72 Commonwealth Ave., 02116/ Tel. (617) 247-8611
Chicago, Illinois—1716 W. Lunt Ave., 60626/ Tel. (312) 973-0900
Cleveland, Ohio—11206 Clifton Blvd., 44102/ Tel. (216) 651-6670
Dallas, Texas—5430 Gurley Ave., 75223/ Tel. (214) 827-6330
Denver, Colorado—1400 Cherry St., 80220/ Tel. (303) 333-5461
Detroit, Michigan—383 Lenox Ave., 48215/ Tel. (313) 824-6000
Gainesville, Florida—214 N.W. 14th St., 32603/ Tel. (904) 336-4183
Gurabo, Puerto Rico—ISKCON, Box HC-01-8441, 00658-9763/ Tel. (809) 737-5222
Hartford, Connecticut—1683 Main St., E. Hartford, 06108/ Tel. (203) 289-7252
Honolulu, Hawaii—51 Coelho Way, 96817/ Tel. (808) 595-3947
Houston, Texas—1320 W. 34th St., 77018/ Tel. (713) 686-4482
Laguna Beach, California—285 Legion St., 92651/ Tel. (714) 494-7029
Lansing, Michigan—1914 E. Michigan Ave., 48912/ Tel. (517) 484-2209
Long Island, New York—197 S. Ocean Ave., Freeport, 11520/ Tel. (516) 867-9045
Los Angeles, California—3764 Watseka Ave., 90034/ Tel. (213) 836-2676
Miami, Florida—3220 Virginia St., 33133/ Tel. (305) 442-7218
New Orleans, Louisiana—2936 Esplanade Ave., 70119/ Tel. (504) 484-6084
New York, New York—305 Schermerhorn St., Brooklyn, 11217/ Tel.(718) 855-6714
New York, New York—26 Second Avenue, 10003
Philadelphia, Pennsylvania—51 West Allens Lane, 19119/ Tel. (215) 247-4600
Philadelphia, Pennsylvania—529 South St., 19147/ Tel. (215) 829-0399
Placentia, California—1022 N. Bradford Ave., 92670/ Tel. (714) 996-7262
St. Louis, Missouri—3926 Lindell Blvd., 63108/ Tel. (314) 535-8085
San Diego, California—1030 Grand Ave., Pacific Beach, 92109/ Tel. (619) 483-2500
San Francisco, California—84 Carl St., 94117/ Tel. (415) 753-8647
San Francisco, California—2334 Stuart St., Berkeley, 94705/ Tel. (415) 644-1113
Seattle, Washington—1420 228th Ave. S.E., Issaquah, 98027/ Tel. (206) 391-3293
Tallahassee, Florida—1323 Nylic St. (mail: P.O. Box 20224, 32304)/ Tel. (904) 681-9258
Tampa, Florida—1205 E. Giddens Ave., 33603/ Tel. (813) 238-9121
Topanga, California—20395 Callon Dr., 90290/ Tel. (213) 455-1658
Towaco, New Jersey—(mail: P.O. Box 109, 07082)/ Tel. (201) 299-0970
Tucson, Arizona—Caitanya Cultural Center, 711 E. Blacklidge Dr., 85719
Walla Walla, Washington—314 E. Poplar, 99362/ Tel. (509) 525-7133
Washington, D.C.—10310 Oaklyn Dr., Potomac, Maryland 20854/ Tel. (301) 299-2100

FARM COMMUNITIES

Alachua, Florida (New Ramana-reti)—Box 819, Alachua, 32615/ Tel. (904) 462-2017
Carriere, Mississippi (New Talavan)—31492 Anner Road, 39426/ Tel. (601) 798-8533
Gurabo, Puerto Rico (New Govardhana Hill)—(contact ISKCON Gurabo)
Hillsborough, North Carolina (New Goloka)—Rt. 6, Box 701, 27278/ Tel. (919) 732-6492
Mulberry, Tennessee (Murari-sevaka)—Rt. No. 1, Box 146-A, 37359/ Tel. (615) 759-7331
Port Royal, Pennsylvania (Gita Nagari)—R.D. No. 1, Box 839, 17082/ Tel. (717) 527-4101

RESTAURANTS

Atlanta—The Hare Krishna Dinner Club (at ISKCON Atlanta)
Chicago—Govinda's Buffet (at ISKCON Chicago)
Dallas—Kalachandji's (at ISKCON Dallas)
Denver—Govinda's Buffet (at ISKCON Denver)
Detroit—Govinda's (at ISKCON Detroit)/ Tel. (313) 331-6740
Eugene, Oregon—Govinda's Vegetarian Buffet, 270 W. 8th St., 97401/ Tel. (503) 686-3436
Laguna Beach, California—Gauranga's (at ISKCON Laguna Beach)
Lansing, Michigan—Govinda's Diners' Club (at ISKCON Lansing)
Los Angeles—Govinda's, 9624 Venice Blvd., Culver City, 90230/ Tel. (213) 836-1269
Miami—(at ISKCON Miami)
Ojai, California—Govinda's Veggie Buffet, 1002 E. Ojai Ave./ Tel. (805) 646-1133
Philadelphia—Govinda's, 521 South Street, 19147/ Tel. (215) 829-0077
Provo, Utah—Govinda's Buffet, 260 North University, 84601/ Tel. (801) 375-0404
St. Louis, Missouri—Govinda's (at ISKCON St. Louis)
San Diego—Govinda's, 3102 University Ave., 92104/ Tel. (619) 284-4826
San Diego—Govinda's at the Beach (at ISKCON San Diego)

San Francisco—Govinda's, 86 Carl St., 94117/ Tel. (415) 753-9703
Santa Cruz, California—Gauranga's, 503 Water St., 95060/ Tel. (408) 427-0294

EUROPE

UNITED KINGDOM AND IRELAND

Belfast, Northern Ireland—140 Upper Dunmurray Lane, Belfast/ Tel. (0232) 681328
Birmingham, England—84 Stanmore Rd., Edgebaston
Dublin, Ireland—3 Temple Lane, Dublin 2/ Tel. (01) 6795887
Leicester, England—21 Thoresby St., North Evington, Leicester/ Tel. (0533) 762587
Liverpool, England—135 Northumberland St., Liverpool, L8 8AY/ Tel. (051) 709 9188
London, England (city)—10 Soho St., London W1V 5FA/ Tel. (071) 437-3662
London, England (country)—Bhaktivedanta Manor, Letchmore Heath, Watford, Hertfordshire WD2 8EP/ Tel. (092385) 7244
Manchester, England—20 Mayfield Rd., Whalley Range, Manchester M16 8FT/ Tel. (061) 226 4416
Newcastle upon Tyne, England—21 Leazes Park Rd./ Tel. (091) 222-0150
Scotland—Karuna Bhavan, Bankhouse Road, Lesmahagow, Lanarkshire/ Tel. (0555) 894790

FARM COMMUNITIES

Hare Krishna Island, N. Ireland—Derrylin, County Fermanagh, BT92 9GN, N. Ireland/ Tel. (03657) 21512
London, England—(contact Bhaktivedanta Manor)

RESTAURANT

London, England—Govinda's, 10 Soho St. / Tel. (071) 437-3662

Krsna conscious programs are held regularly in more than twenty other cities in the U.K. For information, contact Bhaktivedanta Books Ltd., Reader Services Dept., P.O. Box 324, Borehamwood, Herts WD6 1NB/ Tel. (081) 905-1244.

GERMANY

Berlin—Bhakti Yoga Center, Muskauer Str. 27, 1000 Berlin 36/ Tel. (030) 618 92 19
Hamburg—Mühlenstr. 93, 2080 Pinneberg/ Tel. 04101 / 23931
Heidelberg—Kürfursten Anlage 5, D-6900/ Tel. (06221) 15101
Hörup—Neuhörup 1, D-2391 Hörup
Jandelsbrunn, Germany (Nava-Jiyada-Nrsimha-Ksetra)—Zielberg 20, D-8391/ Tel. 85831332
Köln-Gremberg—Taunusstr. 40, 5000 Koln-Gremberg/ Tel. (0221) 830 37 7
Munich—Brodstrasse 12, D-8000 München 82

RESTAURANTS

Berlin—Higher Taste, Kurfuerstendamm 157/158, 1000 Berlin 31/ Tel. (030) 892 99 17
Heidelberg—Higher Taste, Kornmarkt 9, 6900 Heidelberg/ Tel. (06221) 15464

ITALY

Bergamo—Villaggio Hare Krishna, Via Galileo Galilei, 41, 24040 Chignolo D'isola (BG)/ Tel. (035) 490706
Bologna—Via Nazionale 124, 40065-Pianoro (BO)/ Tel. (051) 774-034
Catania—Via San Nicolo al Borgo 28, 95128 Catania, Sicily/ Tel. (095) 522-252
Naples—Via Vesuvio, N33, Ercolano LNA7/ Tel. (081) 739-0398
Rome—Via di Tor Tre Teste 142, 00169 Roma/ Tel. (06) 262913
Vicenza—Via Roma 9, Albettone (Vicenza)

FARM COMMUNITY

Florence (Villa Vrindavan)—Via Communale degli Scopeti 108, S. Andrea in Percussina, San Casciano, Val di Pesa (FI) 5002/ Tel. (055) 820-054

RESTAURANTS

Catania—Govinda's (at ISKCON Catania)
Milan—Govinda's, Via Valpetrosa 3/5, 20123 Milano / Tel. (02) 862-417
Rome—Govinda's, Via di San Simone 73/A, 00186 Roma/ Tel. (06) 654-1973

OTHER COUNTRIES

Amsterdam, Holland—Krishna Dham, 225 Ruysdaelkade, 1072 AW/ Tel.(020) 751 404
Antwerp, Belgium—184 Amerikalei 2000/ Tel. (03) 237-0037, 237-0038
Athens, Greece—Poseidonos 27, Ilioupoli, 16 345/ Tel. (01) 993-7080
Barcelona, Spain—c/de L'Oblit, 67-08026/ Tel. (93) 347-9933
Belgrade, Yugoslavia—Vaisnavska vjerska zajednica, Sumatovacka 118, 11000 Beograd/ Tel. (011) 434-183
Bellinzona, Switzerland—New Nandagram, al Chiossascio, 6594 ContoneTI/ Tel. (092) 622747
Brussels, Belgium—49 rue Marche aux Poulets, 1000 Bruxelles/ Tel. (02) 513 86 05/04
Budapest, Hungary—Hare Krishna Temple, Dimitrov u. 77, Budapest 1028 II, Hungary
Copenhagen, Denmark—Kongens Tvaervej 11, DK-2000 Copenhagen/ Tel. 31868581
Durbuy, Belgium—Chateau de Petit Somme, Durbuy 5482 Tel. (086) 322926
Göthenburg, Sweden—Lagmansgatan 11, s-41653 Göthenburg/ Tel. (031) 192319
Grödinge, Sweden—Korsnäs Gård, 14792 Grödinge/ Tel. (0753) 29151
Helsinki, Finland—Eljaksentie 9, 00370 Helsinki
Lisbon, Portugal—Rua Fernao Lopes, 6, Cascais 2750 (mail: Apartado 2489, Lisbo 1112)/ Tel. (11) 286 713
Ljubljana, Yugoslavia—Kolarjeva 30, 61000 Ljubljana/ Tel. (061) 318-423
Malaga, Spain—Ctra. Alora, 3 int., 29140 Churriana/ Tel. (952) 621038
Malmö, Sweden—Center for Vedisk Kultur, Remegentsgata 14, S-211 42 Malmö/ Tel. (040) 127181
Osafiya, Israel—Hare Krishna, Osafiya 30900/ Tel. (4) 391150
Oslo, Norway—Senter for Krishnabevissthet, Skolestien 11, 0373 Oslo 3
Paris, France—31 Rue Jean Vacquier, 93160 Noisy le Grand/ Tel. (01) 45921018; 43043263
Prague, Czechoslovakia—Hare Krishna, Na Nrazi 5, 18000 Praha 8/ Tel. (02) 821 438
Pregrada, Yugoslavia—Centar za Vedske studije, I Bizek 3, 41090 Zagreb (Podsused), Yugoslavia/ Tel. (041) 190-548
Sarajevo, Yugoslavia—Krajiska 5, 71000 Sarajevo/ Tel. (071) 22-663
Sofia, Bulgaria—Angel Kanchev 34, 1st Floor, Sofia 1000, Bulgaria/ Tel. (02) 878948
Stockholm, Sweden—Fridhemsgatan 22, 11240 Stockholm/ Tel. (08) 549 002
Tel Aviv, Israel—P.O. Box 48163
Turku, Finland—Kaurakatu 39, 20740 Turku 74/ Tel. 358 (9) 21 364 055
Vienna, Austria—Center for Vedic Studies, Rosenackerstrasse 26, 1170 Vienna/ Tel. (0222) 455830
Warsaw, Poland—Mysiadlo k. Warszawy, ul. Zakret 11, 05-500 Piaseczno / Tel. (22) 562-711
Wroclaw, Poland—ul. Buczka 2/18, 50-238 Wroclaw/ Tel. (22)-562-711
Zürich, Switzerland—Bergstrasse 54, 8030 Zürich/ Tel. (01) 262-33-88
Zürich, Switzerland—Preyergrasse 16, 8001 Zürich

FARM COMMUNITIES

Brihuega, Spain (New Vraja Mandala)—(Santa Clara) Brihuega, Guadalajara/Tel. (911) 280018

Chotysany, Czechoslovakia—Krsnuv Dvur c. 1, 257 28 Chotysany

Denmark—Gl. Kirikevej 3, 6650 Broerup/ Tel. 75-392921

Järna, Sweden—Almviks Gård, 15300 Järna/ Tel. (0755) 52050; 52073

Poland (New Santipura)—Czarnow 21, k. Kamiennej gory, woj. Jelenia gora/ Tel. 8745-1892

Roche d'Or, Switzerland—Gokula Project, Vacherie Dessous, 2913 Roche d'Or/ Tel. (066) 766160

Valençay, France (New Mayapur)—Luçay-Le-Mâle, 36 600/ Tel. (054) 40-23-53

RESTAURANTS

Malmö, Sweden—Higher Taste, Amiralsgatan 6, S-211 55 Malmö/ Tel. (040) 970600

Stockholm, Sweden—(at ISKCON Stockholm)

Zürich, Switzerland—Govinda's Restaurant, Preyergasse 16, 8001 Zürich/ Tel. (01) 251-8859

SOVIET UNION

Baku, Azerbaijan—ul. Mikrorayon 123-72, Baku 9, Azerbaijan SSR

Kaunas, Lithuania—Savanoryu 37, 233 000 Kaunas, Lithuanian SSR

Kiev, Ukraine—Kotovskogo 3-39, 252 060 Kiev, Ukrainian SSR/ Tel. (044) 440-7309

Leningrad, Russia—ul. Burtseva 20-147, 20-147 Leningrad/ Tel. (0812) 150-28-80

Minsk, Byelorussia—ul. Pavlova 11, 220 053 Minsk, Byelorussian SSR

Moscow, Russia—Khoroshevskoye shosse d.8, korp.3, 125 284, Moscow/ Tel. (095) 945-4755

Moscow, Russia—Prospekt Mira d.5, kv. 8, Moscow/ Tel. (095) 207-07-38

Novosibirsk, Russia—ul. Leningradskaya 111-20, Novosibirsk

Riga, Latvia—Prospekt Lenina 420-6, 226 024 Riga, Latvian SSR

Sukhumi, Georgia—Pr. Mira 274, Sukhumi, Georgian SSR

Tashkent, Uzbekistan—ul. Babadjanova 36-34, Tashkent, Uzbek SSR

Vladivostok, Russia—ul. Sakhalinskaya 48-12, 690 080 Vladivostok

AUSTRALASIA

AUSTRALIA

Adelaide—74 Semaphore Rd., Semaphore, S. A. 5019/ Tel. (08) 493 200

Brisbane—95 Bank Rd., Graceville, Q.L.D. (mail: P.O. Box 83, Indooroopllly 4068)/ Tel. (07) 379-5455

Canberra—P.O Box 1411, Canberra ACT 2060/ Tel. (06) 290-1869

Melbourne—197 Danks St., Albert Park, Victoria 3206 (mail: P.O. Box 125)/ Tel. (03) 699-5122

Perth—144 Railway Parade (cnr. The Strand), Bayswater (mail: P.O. Box 102, Bayswater, W. A. 6053)/ Tel. (09) 370-1552

Sydney—112 Darlinghurst Rd., Darlinghurst, N.S.W. 2010 (mail: P.O. Box 159, Kings Cross, N.S.W. 2011)/ Tel. (02) 357-5162 or 331-2711

FARM COMMUNITIES

Bambra (New Nandagram)—Oak Hill, Dean's Marsh Road, Bambra, VIC 3241/ Tel. (052) 88-7383

Millfield, N.S.W.—New Gokula Farm, Lewis Lane (off Mt.View Rd. Millfield near Cessnock), N.S.W. (mail: P.O. Box 399, Cessnock 2325, N.S.W., Australia)/ Tel. (049) 98-1800

Murwillumbah (New Govardhana)—Tyalgum Rd., Eungella, via Murwillumbah N. S. W. 2484 (mail: P.O. Box 687)/ Tel. (066) 72-1903

RESTAURANTS

Adelaide—Crossways, 79 Hindley St., Adelaide, S.A. 5000/ Tel. (08) 2315258

Brisbane—Crossways, first floor, 99 Elisabeth Street/ Tel. (07) 210-0255

Melbourne—Crossways, 1st floor, 123 Swanston St., Melbourne, Victoria 3000/ Tel. (03) 650 2939

Melbourne—Gopal's, 139 Swanston St., Melbourne, Victoria 3000/ Tel. (03) 650-1578

North Sydney—Gopal's 180 Falcon St., N. Sydney, N.S.W. 2060/ Tel. (02) 926164

Perth—Hare Krishna Food for Life, 129 Barrack St., Perth, WA 6000/ Tel. (09) 325-2168

Sydney—Govinda's Upstairs and Govinda's Take-away (both at ISKCON Sydney)/ Tel. (075) 501642

NEW ZEALAND AND FIJI

Christchurch, New Zealand—83 Bealey Ave. (mail: P.O. Box 25-190 Christchurch)/ Tel. (3) 61965

Labasa, Fiji—Delailabasa (mail: Box 133)/ Tel. 822912

Lautoka, Fiji—5 Tavewa Ave. (mail: P.O. Box 125)/ Tel. 64112

Rakiraki, Fiji—Rewasa, Rakiraki (mail: P.O. Box 94243)

Suva, Fiji—Nasinu 7 1/2 miles (P.O. Box 6376)/ Tel. 391-282

Wellington, New Zealand—6 Shotter St., Karori (mail: P.O. Box 2753, Wellington)/ Tel. (4) 764445

RESTAURANTS

Auckland, New Zealand—Gopal's, 1st floor., Civic House, 291 Queen St./ Tel. 15 (9) 3034885

Christchurch, New Zealand—Gopal's, 143 Worcester St./ Tel. 67-035

Labasa, Fiji—Govinda's, Naseakula Road/ Tel. 811364

Lautoka, Fiji—Gopal's, Corner of Yasawa St. and Naviti St./ Tel. 62990

Suva, Fiji—Gopal's, 18 Pratt St./ Tel. 62990

Suva, Fiji—Gopal's, 37 Cumming St./ Tel. 312259

FARM COMMUNITY

Auckland, New Zealand (New Varshan)—Hwy. 18, Riverhead, next to Huapai Golf Course (mail: R.D. 2, Kumeu, Auckland)/ Tel. (9) 4128075

AFRICA

Abeokuta, Nigeria—Ibadan Rd., Obantoko, behind NET (mail: P.O. Box 5177)

Abidjan, Ivory Coast—01 BP 8366, Abidjan

Accra, Ghana—582 Blk. 20, Odokor, Official Town (mail: P.O. Box 01568, Osu)

Buea, Cameroon—Southwest Province (mail: c/o Yuh Laban Nkesah, P and T, VHS)

Cape Town, South Africa—17 St. Andrews Rd., Rondebosch 7700/ Tel. (21) 689 1529

Durban (Natal), S. Africa—Chatsworth Centre., Chatsworth 4030 (mail: P.O. Box 56003)/ Tel. (31) 435-815

Freetown, Sierra Leone—13 Bright St., Brookfields (mail: P.O. Box 812, Freetown)

Johannesburg, South Africa—14 Goldreich St., Hillbrow, (mail: P.O. Box 10667, Johannesburg 2000)/ Tel. (11) 484-3629

Kampala, Uganda—Off Gayaza Rd., near Makerere University (mail: P.O. Box 1647, Kampala)

Kisumu, Kenya—P.O. Box 547/ Tel. (035) 42546

Lagos, Nigeria—No. 2 Murtala Mohammed International Airport Expressway, Mafaluku (mail: P.O. Box 8793, Lagos)/ Tel. (01) 966613

Mombasa, Kenya—Hare Krishna House, Sauti Ya Kenya and Kisumu Rds. (mail P.O. Box 82224, Mombasa)/ Tel. 312248

Nairobi, Kenya—Muhuroni Close, off West Nagara Rd. (mail: P.O. Box 28946, Nairobi)/ Tel. 744365

Nkawkaw, Ghana—P.O. Box 69, Nkawkaw

Phoenix, Mauritius—Hare Krishna Land, Pont Fer, Phoenix (mail: P. O. Box 108, Quartre Bornes, Mauritius)/ Tel. (230) 696-5804

Port Harcourt, Nigeria—2 Eligbam Rd. (corner of Obana Obhan St.), G.R.A. II (mail: P.O. Box 4429, Trans Amadi)/ Tel. (084) 330-020
Tokoradi, Ghana—64 Windy Ridge (mail: P.O. Box 328)
Warri, Nigeria—48 Warri-Sapele Rd. (P.O. Box 1922, Warri)/ Tel. (053) 231-859

FARM COMMUNITIES

Mauritius (Vedic Farm)—ISKCON Vedic Farm, Hare Krishna Rd., Beau Bois, Bon Accuel/ Tel. 418-3955

RESTAURANT

Durban, South Africa—Govinda's (contact ISKCON Durban)

ASIA

INDIA

Agartala, Tripura—Assam-Agartala Rd., Banamalipur, 799001
Ahmedabad, Gujarat—Sattelite Rd., Gandhinagar Highway Crossing, Ahmedabad 380 054/ Tel.449945
Bamanbore, Gujarat—N.H. 8A, Surendranagar District
Bangalore, Karnataka—Hare Krishna Hill, 1 'R' Block, Chord Road, Rajajinagar 560 010/ Tel. 359 856
Baroda, Gujarat—Hare Krishna Land, Gotri Rd., 390 015/ Tel. 326299
Bhayandar, Maharashtra—Shivaji Chowk, Station Road, Bhayandar (West), Thane 401101/ Tel. 6091920
Bhubaneswar, Orissa—National Highway No. 5, Nayapali, 751 001/ Tel. 53125
Bombay, Maharashtra—Hare Krishna Land, Juhu 400 049/ Tel. 6206860
Calcutta, W. Bengal—3C Albert Rd., 700 017/ Tel. 473757, 476075
Chandigarh, Punjab—Hare Krishna Land, Dakshin Marg, Sector 36-B, 160 036/ Tel. 44634
Coimbatore, Tamil Nadu—Padmam 387, VGR Puram, Alagesan Road–1, 641-011/ Tel. 45978
Gauhati, Assam—Ulubari Charali, Gauhati 781 001/ Tel. 31208
Guntur, A.P.—Opp. Sivalayam, Peda Kakani 522 509
Hardwar, U.P.—Pahala Mala, Brittany Cottage, Kharkhari 249 401 (mail: P.O. Box 14)
Hyderabad, A.P.—Hare Krishna Land, Nampally Station Rd., 500 001/ Tel. 551018, 552924
Imphal, Manipur—Hare Krishna Land, Airport Road, 795 001/ Tel. 21587
Madras, Tamil Nadu—59, Burkit Rd., T. Nagar, 600 017/ Tel. 443266
Mayapur, W. Bengal—Shree Mayapur Chandrodaya Mandir, P.O. Shree Mayapur Dham, Dist. Nadia/ Tel. 31(Swarup Ganj)
Moirang, Manipur—Nongban Ingkhon, Tidim Rd./ Tel. 795133
Nagpur, Maharashtra—70 Hill Road, Ramnagar, 440 010/ Tel. 33513
New Delhi—M-119 Greater Kailash 1, 110 048/ Tel. 6412058, 6419701
New Delhi—14/63, Punjabi Bagh, 110 026/ Tel. 5410782
Pandharpur, Maharashtra—Hare Krishna Ashram, across Chandrabhaga River, Dist. Sholapur, 413 304
Patna, Bihar—Rajendra Nagar Road No. 12, 800 016/ Tel. 50765
Pune, Maharashtra—4 Tarapoor Rd., Camp, 411 001/ Tel. 60124 and 64003
Secunderabad, A.P.—9-1-1 St. John's Road, 500 026/ Tel. 825232
Silchar, Assam—Ambikapatti, Silchar, Cachar Dist., 788004
Siliguri, W. Bengal—Gitalpara 734 401/ Tel. 26619
Surat, Gujarat—Rander Rd., Jahangirpura, 395 005/ Tel. 84215
Tirupati, A.P.—K.T. Road, Vinayaka Nagar 517 507/ Tel. 20114
Trivandrum, Kerala—T.C. 224/1485, WC Hospital Rd., Thycaud, 695 014/ Tel. 68197
Udhampur, Jammu and Kashmir—Prabhupada Nagar, Udhampur 182 101/ Tel. 496 P.P.
Vallabh Vidyanagar, Gujarat—Sri Sri Radha Giredhari Mandir, opposite Polytechnic College, Vallabh Vidyanagar 338 120
Vrindavana, U.P.—Krishna-Balaram Mandir, Bhaktivedanta Swami Marg, Raman Reti, Mathur Dist. 281 124/ Tel. (5664) 82478

FARM COMMUNITIES

Ahmedabad, Gujarat—Nityananda Seva Ashram, Odhav Rd., Odhav 382 410/ Tel. 886 382
Ahmedabad District, Gujarat—Hare Krishna Farm, Katwada (contact ISKCON Ahmedabad)
Assam—Karnamadhu, Dist. Karimganj
Chamorshi, Maharashtra—78 Krishnanagar Dham, District Gadhachiroli, 442 603
Hyderabad, A.P.—P.O. Dabilpur Village, Medchal Tq., R.R. District, 501 401/ Tel. 552924
Mayapur, W. Bengal—(contact ISKCON Mayapur)

RESTAURANTS

Bombay, Maharashtra—Govinda's (at Hare Krishna Land)
Calcutta—Hare Krishna Karma-Free Confectionary, 6 Russel Street, Calcutta 700 071
Vrindavana—Krishna-Balaram Mandir Guesthouse

OTHER COUNTRIES

Bali, Indonesia—(Contact ISKCON Jakarta)
Bangkok, Thailand—139 Soi Puttha Osotha, New Road (near GPO), Bangkok 10500
Cagayan de Oro, Philippines—30 Dahlia St., Ilaya Carmen, 900 Cagayan de Oro (c/o Sepulveda's Compound)
Chittagong, Bangladesh—Caitanya Cultural Society, Sri Pundarik Dham, Mekhala, Hathazari (city office and mail: 23 Nandan Kanan, Chittagong)/ Tel. 202219
Colombo, Sri Lanka—188 New Chetty St., Colombo 13/ Tel. 33325
Hong Kong—27 Chatam Road South, 6/F, Kowloon/ Tel. 3 7396818
Iloilo City, Philippines—13-1-1 Tereos St., La Paz, Iloilo City, Iloilo/ Tel. 73391
Jakarta, Indonesia—P.O. Box 2694, Jakarta Pusat 10001/ Tel. (21) 4899646
Kathmandu, Nepal—Vishnu Gaun Panchayat Ward No. 2, Budhanilkantha/ Tel. 4-10368
Kuala Lumpur, Malaysia—Lot 9901, Jalan Awan Jawa, Taman Yarl, off 51/2 Mile, Jalan Kelang Lama, Petaling/ Tel. 7830172
Manila, Philippines—170 R. Fernandez, San Juan, Metro Manila/ Tel. 707410
Singapore—Govinda's Gifts, 3 Kerbau Road, Singapore 0718/ Tel. 336-1911 or 339-0109
Taipei, Taiwan—(mail: c/o ISKCON Hong Kong)
Tehran, Iran—Keshavarz-Dehkedeh Ave., Kamran St. No. 58/ Tel. 658870
Tokyo, Japan—2-41-12 Izumi, Suginami-ku, Tokyo T168/ Tel. (03) 3327-1541
Yogyakarta, Indonesia—P.O. Box 25, Babarsari YK, DIY

FARM COMMUNITIES

Bogor, Indonesia—Govinda Kunja (contact ISKCON Jakarta)
Cebu, Philippines (Hare Krishna Paradise)—231 Pagsabungan Rd., Basak, Mandaue City/ Tel. 83254
Perak, Malaysia—Jalan Sungai Manik, 36000 Teluk Intan, Perak

RESTAURANTS

Cebu, Philippines—Govinda's, 26 Sanchiangko St.
Hong Kong—The Higher Taste Vegetarian Dining Club (at ISKCON Hong Kong)
Kuala Lumpur, Malaysia—Govinda's, 16-1 Jalan Bunus Enam Masjid, India/ 03-2986785

LATIN AMERICA

BRAZIL

Belém, PA—Av. Gentil Bittencourt, 1002–Nazare, CEP 66040
Belo Horizonte, MG—Rua St. Antonio, 45, Venda Nova, CEP 31510
Brazilia, DF—Q. 706-Sul, Bloco C, Casa 29, HIGS, CEP 70350/ Tel. (061) 242-7579
Curitiba, PR—Rua Jornalista Caio Machado, 291, B. Sta. Quiteria, CEP 80320
Florianopolis, SC—Rua 14 de julho, 922, Estreito, CEP 88075
Fortaleza, CE—Rua Jose Laurenço, 2114, Aldeota, CEP 60115
Goiania, GO—Rua C-60, Quadra 123, Lt-11, Setor Sudoeste, CEP 74305
Manaus, AM—Avenida 7 de Setembro, 1599, Centro, CEP 69003/ Tel: (092) 232-0202
Pirajui, SP—Av. Brazil, 306, CEP 16600
Porto Alegre, RS—Rua Tomas Flores, 331, Bomfim, CEP 90210
Recife, PE—Rua Reverendo Samuel Falcao, 75, Madalena, CEP 50710
Rio de Janeiro, RJ—Rua Armando Coelho de Freitas, 108, Barra da Tijuca, CEP 22620/ Tel. (021) 399-4493
Salvador, BA—Rua Alvaro Adorno, 17, Brotas, CEP 40240/ Tel: (071) 244-1072
Santos, SP—Rua Nabuco de Araujo, 151, Embare, CEP 11025/ Tel. (0132) 38-4655
São Paulo, SP—Avenida Angelica, 2583, Consolaçao, CEP 01227/ Tel. (011) 59-7352

FARM COMMUNITIES

Caruaru, PE—Comunidade Nova Vrajadhama, Distrito de Murici (mail: CP. 283, CEP 55100)
Pindamonhangaba, SP (Nova Gokula)—Comunidade Nova Gokula, Barrio do Ribeirao Grande (mail: Caixa Postal 067 Pindamonhangaba, SP, CEP 12400)

RESTAURANT

Rio de Janeiro—(at ISKCON Rio)

MEXICO

Guadalajara—Pedro Moreno No. 1791, Sector Juarez/ Tel. (36) 26-58-69
Mexico City—Gob. Tiburcio Montiel No. 45, 11850 Mexico, D.F./ Tel. (5) 271-22-23
Monterrey—Via Pamplona 2916, Col. Mas Palomas/ Tel. (83) 57-09-39
Saltillo—Blvd. Saltillo No. 520, Col. Buenos Aires
Veracruz—Heroes de Puebla No. 85, E/ Tuero Molina y Orizaba, 91910 Veracruz, Ver./ Tel. (29) 37-63-1

FARM COMMUNITY

Guadalajara—Contact ISKCON Guadalajara

RESTAURANTS

Tulancingo—Restaurante Govinda, Calle Juarez 213, Tulancingo, Hgo./ Tel. (775) 3-51-53
Orizaba—Restaurante Radhe, Sur 5 No. 50, Orizaba, Ver./ Tel. (272) 5-75-25

PERU

Arequipa—Jerusalen 402/ Tel. 229523
Cuzco—San Juan de Dios 285
Lima—Pasaje Solea 101 Santa Maria-Chosica/ Tel. 910891
Lima—Schell 634 Miraflores
Lima—Av. Garcilazo de la Vega 1670-1680/ Tel. 259523

FARM COMMUNITY

Hare Krishna-Correo De Bella Vista—DPTO De San Martin

RESTAURANTS

Arequipa—(at ISKCON Arequipa)
Cuzco—Espaderos 128
Lima—Schell 634 Miraflores

OTHER COUNTRIES

Asunción, Paraguay—Centro Bhaktivedanta, Paraguari 469, Asunción/ Tel. 492-800
Bahia Blanca, Argentina—Centro de Estudios Vedicos, Rondeau 473, (8000) Bahia Blanca
Bogotá, Colombia—Calle 63A, #10-62, Chapinero/ Tel. 249-5797
Buenos Aires, Argentina—Centro Bhaktivedanta, Andonaegui 2054, (1431)/ Tel. (01) 515567
Cali, Colombia—Avenida 2 EN, #24N-39/ Tel. 68-88-53
Caracas, Venezuela—Avenida Berlin, Quinta Tia Lola, La California Norte/ Tel. (58-2) 225463
Cochabamba, Bolivia—Av. Heroinas E-0435 Apt. 3 (mail: P. O. Box 2070, Cochabamba)
Cuenca, Ecuador—Entrada de Las Pencas 1– Avenida de Las Americas/ Tel. (593-7) 825211
Essequibo Coast, Guyana—New Navadvipa Dham, Mainstay, Essequibo Coast
Georgetown, Guyana—24 Uitvlugt Front, West Coast Demerara
Guatemala, Guatemala—Apartado Postal 1534
Guayaquil, Ecuador— 6 de Marzo 226 y V. M. Rendon/ Tel. (593-4) 308412 y 309420
La Paz, Bolivia—P. O. Box 10278, Miraflores, La Paz
Montevideo, Uruguay—Centro de Bhakti-Yoga, Pablo de Maria 1427, Montevideo/ Tel. (82) 2484551
Oporto, Portugal—(mail: Apartado 4108, 4002 Porto Codex)
Panama, Republic of Panama—Via las Cumbres, entrada Villa Zaita, frente a INPSA No. 1(mail: P.O. Box 6-29-54, Panama)
Pereira, Colombia—Carrera 5a, #19-36
Quito, Ecuador—Inglaterra y Amazonas
Rosario, Argentina—Centro de Bhakti-Yoga, Paraguay 556, (2000) Rosario/ Tel. 54-41-252630
San José, Costa Rica—Centro Cultural Govinda, Av. 7, Calles 1 y 3, 235 mtrs. norte del Banco Anglo, San Pedro (mail: Apdo. 166,1002)/ Tel. 23-5238
San Salvador, El Salvador—Avenida Universitaria 1132, Media Quadra al sur de la Embajada Americana, San Salvador (mail: P.O. Box 1506)/ Tel. 25-96-17
Santiago, Chile—Carrera 330/ Tel. 698-8044
Santo Domingo, Dominican Republic—Calle Cayetano Rodriquez No. 254
Trinidad and Tobago, West Indies—Orion Drive, Debe/ Tel. 647-739
Trinidad and Tobago, West Indies—Prabhupada Ave. Longdenville, Chaguanas

FARM COMMUNITIES

Argentina (Bhaktilata Puri)—Casilla de Correo No 77, 1727 Marcos Paz, Pcia. Bs.As., Republica Argentina
Bolivia—Contact ISKCON Cochabamba
Colombia (Nueva Mathura)—Cruzero del Guali, Municipio de Caloto, Valle del Cauca/ Tel. 612688 en Cali
Costa Rica—Granja Nueva Goloka Vrindavana, Carretera a Paraiso, de la entrada del Jardin Lancaster (por Calle Concava), 200 metros as sur (mano derecha) Cartago (mail: Apdo. 166, 1002)/ Tel. 51-6752
Ecuador (Nueva Mayapur)—Ayampe (near Guayaquil)
El Salvador—Carretera a Santa Ana, Km. 34, Canton Los Indios, Zapotitan, Dpto. de La Libertad
Guyana—Seawell Village, Corentyne, East Berbice

RESTAURANTS

Cochabamba, Bolivia—Gopal Restaurant, calle Espana N-0250 (Galeria Olimpia), Cochabamba (mail: P. O. Box 2070, Cochabamba)
Guatemala, Guatemala—Callejor Santandes a una cuadra abajo de Guatel, Panajachel Solola
Quito, Ecuador—(contact ISKCON Quito)
San Salvador, El Salvador—25 Avenida Norte 1132
Santa Cruz, Bolivia—Snack Govinda, Av. Argomosa (1ero anillo), esq. Bolivar

SUBSCRIBE TO
BACK TO GODHEAD
The Magazine of the Hare Krishna Movement

Now that you've read *The Laws of Nature: An Infallible Justice*, the importance of Kṛṣṇa consciousness should be apparent. Devotion to Kṛṣṇa is the only way to transcend the twin influences of *kāla* (time) and *karma* (material action and reaction).

Back to Godhead was founded in 1944 by Śrīla Prabhupāda. It is a 64-page bimonthly dedicated to providing knowledge of Kṛṣṇa and the science of Kṛṣṇa consciousness as a means of achieving the highest personal happiness and spiritual fellowship among all living beings. (*continued on next page*)

Bhagavad-gītā As It Is

The world's most popular edition of a timeless classic.

Throughout the ages, the world's greatest minds have turned to the *Bhagavad-gītā* for answers to life's perennial questions. Renowned as the jewel of India's spiritual wisdom, the *Gītā* summarizes the profound Vedic knowledge concerning man's essential nature, his environment, and ultimately his relationship with God. With more than fifty million copies sold in twenty languages, *Bhagavad-gītā As It Is*, by His Divine Grace A. C. Bhaktivedanta Swami Prabhupāda, is the most widely read edition of the *Gītā* in the world. It includes the original Sanskrit text, phonetic transliterations, word-for-word meanings, translation, elaboratc commentary, and many full-color illustrations.

	Pocket	Vinyl	Hard	Deluxe
US	$3.90	$8.50	$10.30	$18.00
UK	£3.00	£5.25	£7.95	£13.95
AUS		$11.00	$14.00	$28.00

The Journey of Self-Discovery

In this collection of illuminating conversations and lectures, Śrīla Prabhupāda leads the reader to a deeper awareness of the self—and the Self.

283 pages

**Soft / US: $4.00; UK: £2.50;
AUS: $5.00**
**Hard / US: $9.95; UK: £7.50;
AUS: $12.00**

A Second Chance

The Story of a Near-Death Experience

As the sinful Ajāmila lay on his deathbed, he was terrified to see three fierce humanlike creatures coming to drag him out of his dying body for punishment. Surprisingly, he was spared. How? You'll find out in the pages of *A Second Chance.*

220 pages

**Soft / US: $4.00; UK: £2.50;
AUS: $5.00**
**Hard / US: $9.95; UK: £7.50;
AUS: $12.00**

Great Vegetarian Dishes

Featuring over 100 stunning full-color photos, this new book is for spiritually aware people who want the exquisite taste of Hare Kṛṣṇa cooking without a lot of time in the kitchen. The 240 international recipes were tested and refined by world-famous Hare Kṛṣṇa chef Kūrma dāsa.

240 recipes, 192 pages, coffeetable size hardback

US: $19.95; UK: £15.95; AUS: $24.95

The Hare Krishna Book Of Vegetarian Cooking

A colorfully illustrated, practical cookbook that not only helps you prepare authentic Indian dishes at home, but also teaches you about the ancient tradition behind India's world-famous vegetarian cuisine.

130 kitchen-tested recipes, 300 pages, hardback

US: $11.60; UK: £8.95; AUS: $15.00

The Higher Taste

A Guide to Gourmet Vegetarian Cooking and a Karma-Free Diet

Illustrated profusely with black-and-white ink drawings and eight full-color plates, this popular volume contains over 60 tried and tested international recipes, together with the why's and how's of the Kṛṣṇa conscious vegetarian life-style.

Softbound, 176 pages

US: $1.99; UK: £1.00; AUS: $2.00

Rāja-Vidyā: The King of Knowledge

In this book we learn why knowledge of Kṛṣṇa is absolute and frees the soul from material bondage.

Softbound, 128 pages

US: $1.00; UK: £1.00; AUS: $2.00

Easy Journey to Other Planets

One of Śrīla Prabhupāda's earliest books, *Easy Journey* describes how *bhakti-yoga* enables us to transfer ourselves from the material to the spiritual world.

Softbound, 96 pages

US: $1.00; UK: £1.00; AUS: $2.00

Beyond Birth and Death

What is the self? Can it exist apart from the physical body? If so, what happens to the self at the time of death? What about reincarnation? Liberation? *Beyond Birth and Death* answers these intriguing questions, and more.

Softbound, 96 pages

US: $1.00; UK: £1.00; AUS: $2.00

The Perfection of Yoga

A lucid explanation of the psychology, techniques, and purposes of *yoga;* a summary and comparison of the different *yoga* systems; and an introduction to meditation.

Softbound, 96 pages

US: $1.00; UK: £1.00; AUS: $2.00

Message of Godhead

An excerpt: "The influences of various people, places, and times have led us to designate ourselves as Hindus, Muslims, Christians, Buddhists, Socialists, Bolsheviks, and so forth. But when we attain transcendental knowledge and are established in *sanātana-dharma,* the actual, eternal religion of the living entity—the spirit soul—then and then only can we attain real, undeniable peace, prosperity, and happiness in the world."

Softbound, 68 pages

US: $1.00; UK: £1.00; AUS: $2.00

Keep in touch . . .

❐ Please send me a free information package, including the small booklet *Kṛṣṇa, the Reservoir of Pleasure* and a catalog of available books.
❐ Bhagavad-gītā As It Is [__Pocket __Vinyl __Hard __Deluxe]
❐ The Journey of Self-Discovery [__Hardbound __Softbound]
❐ A Second Chance [__Hardbound __Softbound]
❐ Great Vegetarian Dishes
❐ The Hare Krishna Book of Vegetarian Cooking
❐ The Higher Taste
❐ Rāja-Vidyā: The King of Knowledge
❐ Easy Journey to Other Planets
❐ Beyond Birth and Death
❐ The Perfection of Yoga
❐ Message of Godhead

Please send me the above books. I enclose $/£____________ to cover the cost and understand that the prices given include postage and packaging.

Name____
PLEASE PRINT

Address______________________________________

City______________________ State____ Zip____________

Mail this form to:

In Europe: The Bhaktivedanta Book Trust, P.O. Box 324, Borehamwood, Herts. WD6 1NB, U.K.

In North America: The Bhaktivedanta Book Trust, 3764 Watseka Ave., Los Angeles, CA 90034, U.S.A.

In Australasia: The Bhaktivedanta Book Trust, P.O. Box 262, Botany, N.S.W. 2019, Australia